DISRUPTOR-IN-CHIEF:

WHY DONALD TRUMP WON AND WHY HE WILL WIN AGAIN

By: Dorollo Nixon, Jr.

Disruptor-In-Chief:
Why Donald Trump Won and Why He Will Win Again

ISBN: 978-0-578-24060-2

CONTENTS

•••••••••●••••••••

A Black Republican Polemic, by Dorollo Nixon, Jr. v

Part I - The Launch..1

    June 16, 2015 3

    725 Fifth Avenue, New York, New York 10022 7

        The Speech 9

        The Great Discontent 16

Part II - The Campaign 23

        Style and Effectiveness 27

        Cleveland, Ohio 31

        The Return of Law and Order 37

Part III - Election Night in America......................................47

        The Walmart Effect 66

        Black, Hispanic, and Asian Voters 71

        Independent Voters..83

        The Money Factor...92

        Immigration 95

Part IV - The Trump Administration, I..................................99

    The Disruptor-in-Chief Takes Office 101

    Washington's Farewell Address 104

Trump's First Inaugural Address: 117
    Themes 118
    Personal Thoughts: President Obama and Chicago 126
Achievements and Set-Backs of Trump's First Administration ...130
Seven Events 133
    Repeal and Replace NAFTA 133
    Repeal and Replace Obamacare 137
    Fighting the Opioid Crisis 141
    Reshaping the Federal Judiciary 144
    China 147
    North and South Korea 149
    Charlottesville, Virginia 151

PART V - Why Trump Will Win Again 159
    Whither America? 161
    Reasons 164
    The Road to Political Slavery 181

Conclusion 209

A Black Republican Polemic,
by Dorollo Nixon, Jr.

· · · · · · ●●● ● ●●●● · · · · ·

Why did a political novice from outside of the bi-partisan Washington D.C. elite win the highest political office in the free world in 2016? Since we Americans are one of the most freedom-loving and immigrant-accepting nations in human history, why did so many of us in Michigan, Iowa, Pennsylvania, and Florida elect a loud-mouth New Yorker with a penchant for bashing outsiders? Finally, why will Donald J. Trump win the presidency a second time in 2020 regardless of whom he faces?

There is no one reason more voters in more places on November 8, 2016, chose Donald Trump instead of Hillary Clinton. And there will not be a singular reason Donald Trump wins the presidency a second time, despite continuing partisan battles with the House of Representatives, the Coronavirus, and the near-collapse of the United States economy. Donald Trump represents different things to different voters who vote for him:

- A successful billionaire businessman
- A champion of conservative values
- A political outsider who will shake up Washington and its stale political culture
- A champion of America and Americans over the rest of the world

- Someone who is not afraid to say what he thinks and feels
- An orange-haired middle finger to the Establishment

Do not look for unity among these points of view; there may not be one.

Where do we look for answers? We must begin by looking at what happened to middle class families across America over the past twenty-five to thirty years. During that time frame for the first time in almost a century Americans ended up poorer rather than richer; economic opportunities for persons without a four year college degree - *most* of the adult population - dwindled as more jobs were sent overseas. Stable working communities throughout middle America that had once formed the bedrock of our nation collapsed under the weight of drug addiction and despair. Yet during that same timeframe America produced more wealthy people than ever before. Our system produced more billionaires faster than anywhere except Beijing and Moscow. Many of these new wealthy people are foreign-born and came to our country to attend university or pursue graduate degrees which have been one gateway to higher paying jobs. What is the significance of these two facts when most of the country has gotten worse off? Meanwhile, the cost of everything that matters to middle Americans - healthcare, a house, an education for our children, safety - kept rising out of reach. Discontent with "the Clintons and the Bushes" was rising. America was slipping out of reach. What was needed - politically, economically, socially, emotionally - was disruption. Here we find the unifying circumstances, values, interests and fears that turned what appeared at first like a publicity stunt into a presidency.

Donald Trump disrupted the 2016 Presidential Race. His campaign revealed he has an uncanny ability to pick issues many Americans care about, state his disrupting viewpoint, and articulate a rationale that would sell beyond Trump's base. As it turned out, that was enough to propel a political novice into the most powerful political office on the planet. But will it be enough to pull off another coup d'etat at the ballot/mail box?

This investigation is worth the effort, because Donald J. Trump will win another term in office in 2020. Why am I so certain? Because the circumstances, values, interests, and fears among voters in America's middle ranks will demand it. The progressives, the liberals, for all their passionate urging, operate under a fundamental misunderstanding - a misunderstanding about what America was created to do. They think America exists to help (force) humanity to advance into some state of the ideal society. But America exists to set people free from unrepresentative, unilateral, arbitrary action. When we do that we live up to our DNA. And when we enslave people, when we bureaucratize and standardize societal behavior and remove choice and dissent (e.g. "only school lunches and school uniforms allowed"), when we treat people differently based on whatever category they fall into rather than uphold their rights as individuals, we betray our fundamental organizing purpose.

I am a conservative African American. I have been a Republican for more than twenty years. How is that even possible, some readers ask? Where have you been all my life, other readers exclaim? That is America. (For the record, I was in upstate New York.)

I possess a unique perspective on Donald Trump's first presidential campaign, because I was heading my own political campaign that same year. I was running to represent my community in the New York State Assembly. I saw firsthand the impact Donald Trump's words and actions had. I also saw the grim reality of many people in our community after thirty years of bad economic news and poor government policy decisions. They had few choices left. But they knew who would fight for them.

After Donald Trump's surprising victory, I quickly became aware that many well-educated, successful people were clueless about why he had won. They were quick to fall for every liberal smokescreen offered up by the Democratic Party leadership in the House of Representatives. As the years of his first administration rolled by and President Trump executed more and more of what he said he intended to do, I came to the conviction that he would win again. No matter what. And no matter who faced off against him.

This book is my perspective as an American on the political events of the past five years, which say so much about the future of our great country.

PART I

$$\cdots\cdots\cdots\bullet\!\bullet\!\bullet\!\Large\bullet\!\normalsize\bullet\!\bullet\cdots\cdots\cdots$$

THE LAUNCH

June 16, 2015

●●●●●●●●●●●●●●●●

Summer in New York: incredibly hot, noisy, hurried. In midtown and in most other parts of Manhattan, crowds of people rush by throughout the business day, though not everyone is working. Tourists, students, beggars and the homeless mix pell-mell with bankers, artists, shopworkers, construction workers and men and women doing countless other things to make a dollar. A thousand conversations generate enough buzz almost to drown out the revving motors in the streets. Underneath, the screech and rumble of the subway provides the bass line.

Most men are dressed in navy or grey, but here and there, streaks of color flash: red, orange, violet, lavender, kelly green. Patterns emerge and then dissipate. Somehow, no one looks the same, even the suits.

They come from all over America and all over the world to be here in Manhattan in the center of it all. Many are dreamers, borne here by an idea, an emotion, a vision of themselves that Kansas or Milwaukee or even Los Angeles could not flesh out. Let alone overcrowded cities and dying villages throughout the Third World. They have come to the place where anything is possible. But most of these people are practical, bottom line-driven realists. Here is the deal: take it or leave it.

Sometime during the middle of the day in the heart of midtown, a man descended in an elevator to the atrium of a sleek black tower. He was wearing a navy suit. Or perhaps it was black. It does not matter. Everyone in New York knew his name. But few people knew the man behind the name. Despite decades of media attention he remained an enigma.

He stepped out of the elevator and walked over to a podium. A crowd was waiting for him to speak. There were television cameras pointed at him. Some of the crowd held signs in their hands. No one knew what he was going to say. Did he?

The words he spoke that day changed the entire world.

***

Cursory research would show that over the past thirty years Donald Trump had made several statements about U.S. politics and policies, as well as some forays into presidential politics. Not municipal politics in the City of New York; not state politics in Albany, New York's capital. Just presidential politics. Apparently, only the big time interests Donald Trump, which is both fitting, given his outsize personality and image, and self-serving. A man like Donald Trump only wants to come in at the top.

Even at this early point in the summer of 2015, the year before the actual presidential election, *eleven* other Republican candidates were already in the running, with several others to follow in the next forty days. The eleven included three sitting governors, three active U.S. Senators, three former governors, a world famous pediatric neurosurgeon and a former tech CEO. One was female, one was Black, two were Hispanic.

One of the stronger candidates was the U.S. Senator from Florida, Marco Rubio, a young conservative Republican whose grandparents came to the United States from Cuba. Fluent in Spanish and English, Senator Rubio had a track record of electoral victories and policy positions that set him apart from the other candidates and gave him weapons in a fight against Democrats, who usually dominate the Hispanic vote.

But preeminent among the candidates was former governor of Florida, Jeb Bush. Standing above his peers at six feet five inches tall (the only candidate taller than Donald Trump), Jeb was the son and brother of two living U.S. presidents and the grandson of a U.S. Senator. Wealthy and with great name recognition, Jeb began the presidential campaign in the lead. However, he had more to offer than just being a Bush and money. Jeb's longtime wife is a Mexican immigrant. The racism she experienced in Houston, TX, where the Bush family has been based for around seventy years, was so strong Jeb moved his family to Florida. Fluent in Spanish and English, with offspring whose skin color is brown, not white, Jeb could engage with Hispanic voters in an impactful way and still tout Republican values.

Two times Jeb Bush had won the gubernatorial election in Florida, now the third most populous U.S. state. In fact, Jeb had never lost a political election in his life. He came to the table with organizational leadership, fundraising experience and a network of political supporters which was a hundred years old. Jeb demonstrated this by raising more than $100 million in campaign donations within the first seven days.

I was not impressed by Donald Trump when I learned he had entered the presidential race, but I was very impressed by Governor Bush.

But It turned out Trump had already sowed the seeds of Bush's political destruction and he had sowed them in a field whose harvest was decades in the making.

725 Fifth Avenue, New York, New York 10022

•••••••••●•••••••••

If you're riding in the back of a taxi or an Uber you might miss it. There are so many other buildings like it that line Fifth Avenue between Fifty-Seventh Street and Fiftieth Street, where one catches a brief glimpse of Rockefeller Center before being boxed in once again by more skyscrapers. When one reaches Forty-Second Street and the expanse of cerulean and poplar created by the Lennox Library (as it used to be called), there is Bryant Park and open space in the heart of America's most crowded city.

Each skyscraper is a unique reflection of the man (usually), woman, family, corporation or investment group that spent hundreds of millions or billions of dollars to hang their dreams in the sky for everyone to see. Each one has not only its own story but its own myth. Trump Tower is no different.

Massive, black, glistening and graceful, Trump Tower rising fifty-seven floors above the east side of the avenue. On the other side of the street and three blocks down is a hundred-year-old stone Episcopalian church. Nearby buildings include luxury clothing stores, world-renowned jewelers, and the Carlyle Hotel, one of President John F. Kennedy's secret haunts. Donald Trump could not have chosen a better location for the center of his universe. Thus it is only fitting he launched his first political campaign here.

Trump Tower contains a five-story atrium whose centerpiece is a sixty foot internal waterfall. The cascading flows catch the eye; the gentle splash below soothes the tourist or patron passing through and obscures conversations from neighbors.

What one sees is a gaudy spectacle of extravagant luxury. It leaves the audience to gape and gawk, to be bowled over by this atrium and we naturally turn inwardly to consider the man who "built" this from nothing. The man who built himself from nothing.

This is the myth of Trump Tower.

Without doubt Donald Trump planned for this effect from before ground was broken on the building back in 1979 ; Donald Trump is the consummate entertainer. He knows what people want, he knows what works and what doesn't. The experts? They're idiots in the Trumpverse, even when the Donald stoops to rely on them. This is utility without respect. What the Donald respects, though, is the audience.

By the time Donald Trump arrived in his atrium the audience was buzzing with anticipation. The visual highlight of the entire event was the moment Trump and his wife, former model Melania Knavs, and the rest of his personal retainers descended to the atrium's floor via the escalator.

A moving staircase is a fixture of practically every shopping mall in America, especially urban shopping centers like the one located in Trump Tower, to maximize space vertically instead of horizontally. In American culture, a staircase has cultural meaning beyond its function.

For Americans a staircase represents upward mobility, the ability to begin in one place socially and geographically and rise to a higher level. Poets, novelists, screenwriters and movie producers have used this trope for more than a century to evoke the potential inherent in the American experiment.

Even though Donald Trump used the escalator to descend rather than rise, the inherent symbolism could not be missed. Surely it was handcrafted in every detail. There was the added power of an effortless descent - unworked for, gracious, almost "Olympian". Trump came down to the masses, blessing them with his presence, his physical presence more than with his words even.

His moment had finally come and Donald Trump arrived at the center of the Trumpverse. The Donald was at the center of it all, all eyes on him, the Producer, the Spinner, the Showman. The moment had come to deliver the unexpected.

The Speech

In American politics both historically and today the most powerful weapon is a speech. Speeches establish who a candidate is, outline his or her agenda and solicit buy-in from voters. Moreover, speeches far outlast candidates.

Take Abraham Lincoln as a case in point. While President Lincoln is known for ending slavery, he is relevant in this context because he is remembered for his words. Four speeches - the 1858 House Divided speech at the Illinois state capitol, Lincoln's First Inaugural Address in 1861, the Gettysburg Address, and Lincoln's Second Inaugural forty-one days prior to his tragic death - fixed in stone until eternity who Lincoln was and what he stood for politically.

His august words, clarity of vision, and breadth of humanity can neither be lost or missed because we possess to this day original copies of his own drafts or copies made viva voce as he spoke. In this way, Lincoln's speeches continue to attest to how great he was as a man, a politician and an American.

Other great presidents in the American pantheon and even some good ones have left speeches which continue to ring loudly the notes of freedom, justice, liberty, and equality down through the ages. Presidents Franklin D. Roosevelt and John F. Kennedy were not the only ones. Their peers in oratory include Andrew Jackson, Teddy Roosevelt and even George W. Bush who, standing on a pile of rubble with a megaphone in hand and the still smoldering ruins of the myth of American untouchability behind him, used his blunt, plain spoken manner akin to President Harry Truman to reassure all Americans and their allies that whoever did this would pay. Swiftly.

Ironically, the effects of the ever-increasing power of radio, television and internet media on political speeches has been largely negative. While these forms of media vastly increased the potential real-time audience for a political speech, they have somehow decreased the power of oratory. One might argue the practitioners of oratory merely have less ability, or that their speechwriters are less skilled. I do not agree. Somehow, the power to watch, analyze and follow political speeches from a couch in front of a television cheapens, diminishes or trivializes oratory.

Bringing us once again to Donald Trump.

On June 16, 2015, Donald Trump gave one of the clumsiest but most effective political speeches in recent American history. It was discursive, self-serving and vulgar. But it explained clearly that Trump understood what was fundamentally wrong with America;

he was not afraid to say it. And he would do - not just "propose" - big things that would change the future for all Americans.

Donald Trump - or whoever wrote this speech, for we do not know - organized the speech as one long indictment of the bipartisan political elite who have been running America into the ground for the last three decades.

What was Donald Trump's methodology? It was straight outta Queens: trash talking. The billionaire businessman began his speech by trashing the political and economic effectiveness of current U.S. policy. It reads like a juvenile diatribe of our political leaders. However, if one continues to pay attention, one sees Trump's ideas become more concrete; his frustrations coalesce into sound judgments about the state of America in 2015. The *coups de grace* were Donald Trump's campaign promises. These demonstrate that this speech was not some off-the-cuff rant or public brainstorming exercise, but was a well thought out piece of political rhetoric. In his very first campaign speech, Donald Trump established all of the essentials of his successful presidential campaign platform. Both the core ideas he stood for and the outrageous extremes that would grab much air time, they are all there.

Donald Trump's opening slavos included a reference to the United States being "$18 trillion" in debt. Whose fault was it? China. "They're ripping us off," said new first time presidential Candidate Donald Trump. But at the same time, "I love China," followed by reference to a business deal with unnamed Chinese persons. This was not the only place in his launch speech that contained an irrepressible selfish plug.

Donald Trump also laid the blame squarely at the feet of the bipartisan status quo running America's government. "Our leaders are stupid." They don't know what they're doing. "They don't know business." "They don't know how to negotiate." Mexico? "They [sic] are not our friend." They send us people with problems. Drug problems. Crime problems. "They are rapists. And some, I assume, are good people." Was this seriously a diagnosis of America's most important political problems? Or was this a sixth grader fighting with a classmate on the middle school playground?

On and on he went: Obamacare is a "big lie" and a "disaster" that will make healthcare costs skyrocket; China and the oil cartel are smarter than our leaders. The audience of journalists probably enjoyed Donald Trump's performance. It was newsworthy and entertaining. At some point early on, I bet, they stopped taking in the details.

How did Doanld Trump sum up almost fifteen years of U.S. Middle Eastern policy? "We have nothing. We can't even go there." According to Trump, the U.S. spent $2 trillion, lost thousands of American lives, destabilized the region, promoted the rise of ISIS ("They built a hotel"), and left thousands of humvees which our enemies appropriated. To top it off, Donald Trump claimed he had spoken out against these ventures in the beginning.

What was Donald Trump's take on the U.S. economy? Here it is verbatim:

> Last quarter, it was just announced our gross domestic product— a sign of strength, right? But not for us. It was below zero. Whoever heard of this? It's never below zero. Our labor participation rate was the worst since 1978. But think of it, GDP below zero, horrible labor participation rate.

According to Forbes Magazine, 1Q 2015 GDP was 0.2%. The same publication stated that 2Q 2015 GDP (which came out about one month after Trump's speech) was 2.3%. That is not zero, *a fortiori* "below zero." It turned out, though, that in a prescient manner, facts did not matter in the Trumpverse. What mattered was how Donald Trump made you feel. For cross reference: during the 1992 Presidential Campaign then former Arkansas Governor William Jefferson Clinton declared famously, "I feel your pain" and went on to become a two-term U.S. president with a defensible record of spending cuts and economic growth for Wall Street and the upper middle class.

Donald Trump claimed that the United States spent money on seven major things: China, Japan, Saudi Arabia, public education, Iraq, and entitlements. And what did we get? Ripped off, trillions more in debt, endless wars we don't win, school performance that lags behind the rest of the Western world, Social Security on the brink of bankruptcy, a poorly equipped military, and rotting infrastructure not fit for a first world nation.

And what of President Obama? Here is Donald Trump, verbatim:

> You know, when President Obama was elected, I said, "Well, the one thing, I think he'll do well. I think he'll be a great cheerleader for the country. I think he'd be a great spirit." He was vibrant. He was young. I really thought that he would be a great cheerleader.

> He's not a leader. That's true. You're right about that. But he wasn't a cheerleader. He's actually a negative force. He's been a negative force. He wasn't a cheerleader; he was the opposite.

Hardly a racist slur of America's first Black president.

What did Donald Trump say about his fellow Republicans running for the nomination? "They're wonderful people," but they cannot negotiate, because they do not know what they are doing and they are beholden to lobbyists and special interests. According to Trump, if Ford Motor Company announced that it intended to open a plant in Mexico, none of his competitors would be able to stop it. But Donald Trump, who characterized himself in this speech as a "free trader," would put a stop to it with the threat of tariffs.

Through these discursive forays into one topic after another, Donald Trump's ideas coalesced into solid political statements: many Americans cannot find jobs because the jobs all went abroad, and elite politicians will not talk about jobs or the damage China has done to the United States in the twenty-first century. Massive amounts of government spending go to the wrong people (some of whom are very bad people) and do not achieve results. We are ignoring people and problems back home while engaged in endless, costy crusades abroad. Free trade is fine, but U.S. trade deals were poorly negotiated.

How did Donald Trump propose to solve these significant social and economic problems when the political elite and the candidates it spawned were powerless to effect change? By offering himself, of course. "We need a leader that wrote 'The Art of the Deal," said Trump unselfconsciously.

Trump went on to make the case for himself as the only candidate in the bunch. He touted his business acumen and negotiating skills. Trump practically gushed about his net worth. He claimed it would make him independent of special interests. He literally talked about how much money he claims he is worth. Certainly this was the vulgar low-point of his announcement speech.

And then to wind up, Donald Trump made a series of campaign promises. All politicians do this. We promise potential voters that if we are elected we will do something they like. Or hurt someone they don't like. We do it to induce them to vote for us. But that is not what Donald Trump did.

Donald Trump used braggadocio and bluster in his speech to sway people to support him. He sold himself as the Problem Solver-in-Chief. But he did not sell his ideas. Those were his own. When he finally revealed them to the general public through this speech whatever someone might say about them, they could not say that they were not his own. Ironically for a man who struggles with facts he does not like, this gave Donald Trump an integrity and a power he could unleash against political opponents.

Donald Trump promised that if elected he would repeal and replace Obamacare; build the wall; be tough on ISIS; make the military tough again; stop Iran from getting nuclear weapons; end President Obama's "illegal" executive order on immigration; "fully support and back up the Second Amendment;" end common core; rebuild the country's infrastructure; "*save medicare, medicaid and social security without cuts*;" renegotiate foreign trade deals; reduce our debt; take care of our vets.

These promises took Trump well past the Republican trope of tax cuts. Trump promised to restructure fundamentally the status quo of federal government action in the United States. And he promised to renegotiate our relationships aboard. Only Israel, apparently, was in a special category. In other words, Donald Trump promised to disrupt the corrupt social and economic contract foisted on Middle America by a self-serving coastal elite twenty-five years before.

Recall that earlier in this chapter I identified that strong, effective political speeches begin with the Big Why. Donald Trump ended his announcement speech with his Big Why:

> Sadly, the American dream is dead. But if I get elected president I will bring it back bigger and better and stronger than ever before, and we will make America great again

Standing in the atrium of Trump Tower, with the media before him, no one could doubt Donald Trump's successes up to that moment. He owned hotels, casinoes, golf courses, and other real estate on several continents. He had made hundreds of millions of dollars producing multiple different types of entertainment acts, from heavyweight championship boxing matches to the Miss Universe pageant to a popular primetime television show. But when Donald Trump evoked the death of the American dream, Middle America felt the pain. The next section of the book will explore that pain and the discontent it created, which proved to be the most dominant factor in the 2016 presidential election for both Republicans and Democrats.

The Great Discontent

Between 1990 and 2015 - the entire post-Cold War era - the average American household got poorer rather than richer. Correct. And this was the case despite relatively sound government spending practices. During the Clinton Administration (1993-2001), the federal government balanced its budget, reduced government spending (including military spending) and enjoyed tax surpluses and a rising stock market. Meanwhile, during the middle of these years the United States entered into trade relationships with neighbors Canada and Mexico to form the North American Free Trade Agreement (NAFTA), effectively turning all of North America into the most powerful free-trade zone on earth at that time. NAFTA eased the movement of goods and capital across U.S. borders. However, importantly, it did not provide for free movement of people the way the Treaty of Maastricht did in the European Economic Community in 1993. U.S. capital could move into Mexico and Canada, buying assets and manufacturing goods at lower labor costs, which were then shipped back into the United States to be sold to American consumers. To some it sounded ideal. But American workers, especially in manufacturing, began losing their high salary, high benefit jobs and found it difficult to secure work for similar compensation. Tech innovation began to pick up speed towards the end of that decade and this only made the circumstances for many American workers worse.

The Bush Administration (2001-2009) further increased the pressure on American workers. The federal government began to run deficits again. Bush increased entitlement spending (i.e., federal medical or social welfare spending which is non-discretionary) by expanding Medicare to cover certain prescription drugs for senior citizens. And, famously, President George Bush took us to war against Saddam Hussein's Iraq and against the Taliban in Afghanistan. U.S. troops remain in both of those countries today.

Meanwhile, domestically, the stock markets rallied from 2005-2008; unemployment fell and GDP rose. However, manufacturing - the backbone of the American working class and for much of the middle class - continued to decline in favor of imported goods mostly from China. The U.S. ran up a colossal trade deficit with China to the tune of hundreds of billions of dollars each year.

Thus when the subprime mortgage-backed securities market historically collapsed in 2008, causing a world-wide cash shortage as banks and investors sought return of capital from funds which were virtually empty because the assets were now worthless, the U.S. government and the U.S. middle class were in poor positions to respond. The 2008 Subprime Mortgage Crisis and Great Recession consumed trillions of dollars of retiree's assets and wiped out pension fund account balances - a loss of a *lifetime's* worth of labor. Not a single major player or even a middle manager from the financial sector went to jail over what arguably was a massive fraud on the American consumer.

In November 2008, then Senator Barack Hussein Obama was elected to the highest office in the land. He was the very first African American to win the presidency. He took over managing the country's recovery from the financial crisis. Slowly, asset values began to rise again in the real estate sector and other industries. Stock indices rose to new highs. But this only helped middle class Americans who did not lose their jobs or their homes as a result of the financial crisis. Unemployment, which rose to 12% - its highest level in America since the Great Depression eighty years earlier - began to fall. But for many middle class Americans, a good paying job that supported a family for years had been wiped; they adjusted to other work for less pay and less benefits* . Thus the recovery, for many, especially during its first four years, only happened on paper: there was little immediate tangible improvement in their circumstances. Additionally, while unemployment did decrease, so did the labor participation rate. This will be important when discussing Trump's appeal to get Americans back to work.

Further, President Obama succeeded in getting Congress to pass his signature domestic "reform," nicknamed Obamacare. This was a comprehensive overhaul of the U.S. health insurance market. While some aspects of this law were very popular - i.e., the prohibition of insurance companies from refusing to insure consumers with pre-existing chronic medical conditions which would cost insurance companies more money - Obamacare famously mandated that all adult Americans and permanent residents purchase insurance coverage. This aspect of the law was challenged in the federal courts as unconstitutional. A divided U.S. Supreme Court, the last practical arbiter within the United States on what the U.S. Constitution requires or prohibits, upheld the law as constitutional... by characterizing it as a tax. Congress's power to tax U.S. citizens, while less expansive than a state legislature's taxing power, still comes well within its constitutional powers. However, the Supreme Court's decision did nothing to improve the law's popularity.

For many middle class Americans (almost all of whom already had health insurance coverage through work, through their spouse's work, or through their parents*) Obamacare was one more federal government imposition on their economic circumstances. Household budgets which already had to cope with job losses and increased costs of goods and services now had to grapple with further increases in the costs of insurance.

Moreover, between 1997 and 2015, federal spending expanded 800%***, decimating the buying power of retired middle class Americans who live on fixed incomes with little or no cost-adjustment. According to the Economic Policy Institute, wage growth of earners in the 50th percentile rose only 6% from 1997 to 2013, crippling the ability of working Americans to invest in education to improve their economic circumstances, to buy real estate - the chief asset of the U.S. middle class - and to handle random, high costs health emergencies, which could place otherwise debt-free Americans in debt to tax-free "nonprofit" healthcare companies for the rest of their lives.

These trends hit young Americans very hard. Even the college educated did not escape. According to the Economic Policy Institute, college grads aged twenty-one to twenty-four earned almost the same average amount in 1998 and 2013: $16.34 and $16.99. However, when expressed in constant 2013 dollars, the damage done by massive government spending, wage stagnation and the Great Recession is manifest: $16 in 1998 was the equivalent of $22.78 in 2013. For a full time worker, this represented a loss of more than *$40 per day!*

And then Donald Trump took an elevator ride down to the atrium of Trump Tower, opened his mouth, and changed all of that.

Donald Trump's announcement speech was calculated to reach immediately into the hearts of middle class Americans who, over twenty-five years, had seen their dreams shattered and their destinies hijacked by an overspending, intrusive federal government that allowed an irresponsible financial sector to destroy American prosperity. Trump's vision of the U.S. in 2015 largely described what they saw and experienced: crumbling roads, dilapidated airports, closed factories, outsourced jobs. Who was to blame? Hillary Clinton, NAFTA, globalism, China and special interests. Anyone but them.

This critique, like an arrow, struck home in Middle America. Voters on the coasts, especially upper middle class ones, might have experienced great growth and opportunity during the 1990's and 2000's. But once one moves inland by about sixty miles, every town with more than 30,000 people had seen at least one factory close; the average regional airport was in poor shape; and tourists who visited the U.S. each year could attest to how poor our bridges and road infrastructure looked.

Donald Trump promised to disrupt this reality. He promised to repeal and replace what America had become with a stronger, better version of the nation. Tens of millions of voters took him at his word. As the next chapter shows, Donald Trump campaigned hard to make it a reality.

Personal Note:
I was not present when Donald Trump gave his stump speech. I was about 200 miles away in upstate New York, where I live and work. Either a news article online, on Facebook or in a newspaper told me that Donald Trump had joined the Republican presidential field.

My first reaction was incredulous laughter. He can't be serious - that's what went through my mind. And I certainly thought that Trump would never win. He could not because he wasn't a politician; voters would never take his candidacy seriously.

Looking back, I was unaware of the depth of discontent in America with the political status quo. Millions upon millions of voters in both the Democratic and Republican parties were fed-up with traditional politics and standard-issue politicians. After twenty-five years of economic retreat and loss by the middle class, the game was up.

The same persons on the stage saying the same things would no longer get elected. In fact, they would no longer even be able to drive the campaign narrative.

PART II

THE CAMPAIGN

・・・・・・●●●●●●●●・・・・・・

Donald Trump is a beast. He is a carnivore. He devours his opponents. He also wears them down with his tenacity. Trump is an unorthodox disruptor. He chose paths and means which others shunned or did not see. The Trump presidential campaign demonstrated these dynamics of Trump's personality more than any other aspect of his life, business or administration.

United States presidential campaigns are a series of public events followed by a primary (vote), a convention selection (vote) between June to August, and the general election (vote) in November. There are four basic presidential campaign events: speeches, debates, town hall meetings, and hustings. The above list is in order of precedence, moving from most-controlled to least-controlled. A candidate standing on a stump (stage, floor, atrium) speaking his or her mind on the relevant issues is classic politics in a democracy. Here they have the most control of their interactions with the public. The candidate can best craft an image to leave in the minds of voters through speeches. Hustings are the complete opposite: a candidate attends community events scheduled by others in a place that is not the candidate's home. Just about anyone can approach the candidate, ask questions, take photos, accost, shout-down, get arrested, etc.

The votes are either called a primary or a caucus. Usually the voters of only a particular party have the right to participate in that party's primary. Party voters choose which candidate they desire to be nominated by their party at the convention. By winning a given primary, a candidate wins a certain number of delegates (nominated by the state party) who will attend the midsummer party convention.

After the convention, the party's chosen nominee repeats the same campaign events across the country in a manner of his or her own choosing, culminating in the national election in early November.

Donald Trump's now infamous campaign event is a stadium rally. Trump's team selects a location in the target state. The locations seem to be always in the margins. Capital cities and major metropolitan areas are mostly ignored. This is not an accident.

These out-of-the-way locations are part of a strategy to reach into the heart of America - the Midwest, the South, Texas, the Mountain West, and the MidAtlantic. While this appears to be polyvalent, lying at the base are the same foundations: family, small town, small business, and community. The heartland embraces places throughout the country where communities suffer the slowest rate of breakdown. By locating his campaign rallies in these places, Trump had his finger on the pulse of the nation.

The coastal cities, by contrast, are places that catalyse the breakdown of traditional community in the name of individual liberty and economic independence. Each of them have their own traditional community, many of which are longstanding. However, the concentrating, aggregating effect of cities overrides community. Residents in coastal cities accept the displacement of traditional culture as cities experience high amounts of in-migration, many residents moving there for that purpose. It is a choice to substitute one set of values oriented towards maximizing individual choice as a means of order for a set of values that seeks to limit individual choice for the purpose of maintaining an order centered around a rooted notion of family, place and identity.

Style and Effectiveness

TV debates. Donald Trump debating other presidential candidates was a cross between a boxing match and a comedy show. Trump was remembered more for his personal insults and the reactions these caused than for any policy initiative he announced. This made Donald Trump unique not merely because he won the Repubican nomination and then won the election. Every other candidate on stage talked about what they wanted to accomplish and why, the problems facing our country, their personal set of skills for the job. In contrast, Donald Trump stood there glowering at everyone. Then he would open his mouth and dish out rancor and invective. Shocking, yes, but it was effective at calling into question not merely the fitness of the other candidates, but also the fitness of the elites that produced those candidates; the elites who stage-managed the debate process and the election itself; the elites who have been stage-managing America for their own interests and against the interests of most middle class Americans.

America only suffers elites to rule when those elites serve the interests of the non-elite middle class. And they must do so from the shadows. If the processes of control become too visible Americans will instinctually reject the elite.

Further, Trump was uncontrollable. He demanded things go his way and he did not give a damn what anyone else thought. Perhaps this was merely bad manners. But my gut says it was much more than that. No one who is nice will win a fight in a prison yard or on a playground. Nice earns you a whupping. Projecting strength and aggressive confrontation from a position of strength - that will make the others back off. Ultimately, though, as former undisputed, undefeated heavyweight boxing champion Iron Mike Tyson put it so elegantly, "Everyone has a plan until they get hit in the face."

Trump hits you in the face. First. Very hard. And he never lets up.

A blustering, racist buffoon may be what you see and hear, but the reality is that Donald Trump is a skillful businessman who is comfortable and confident fighting for what he wants. This is true whether the goal is building a new hotel, contesting a property tax assessment, negotiating a supply contract, starring in his own reality TV show, or being President of the United States.

Trump repeatedly stated scathing truths other politicians would not dare say.

Throughout his presidential campaign, Donald Trump promised to return "the American dream" to the middle class - hardworking people whose wages have not risen to match the rising costs of housing, education and healthcare during the past thirty years.

The Clintonian alternative was telling and filled with contempt - nothing is wrong with our country. Now go back to work.

It was not so much the speeches Senator Hillary Rodham Clinton gave across the country but the ethos of the campaign and behind-the-scenes actions of her campaign and national Democratic party insiders that left a bad taste in everyone's mouth. This was especially so for supporters of Senator Bernie Sanders, many of whom felt betrayed by their own party. Recall that as of 2016, the Democratic National Convention still contained a superdelegate voting structure to permit the party elite to basically choose whichever nominee it wanted.

Trump viewed with contempt *all* of America's political elite, both Republicans and Democrats who sold out their hard working, middle class fellow citizens for huge profits. Trump is extremist. Trump is ridiculous, and ridiculous sells. He got more media time for free than any other candidate by shocking people with his views and being ridiculous.

Trump thinks twelve moves ahead, and he employs a Walmart Strategy. The Walton family became the richest family on Earth by locating its supermarkets within the United States (the world's biggest consumer market) in marginal, out of the way places where there was little competition. Then they ruthlessly drove the price of goods to the floor. Who could resist? People with money and taste; people with options. Fortunately for the Waltons, and later for Donald J. Trump, that was not most Americans. Nor had it ever been.

When I was in high school and Cornell University during the 1990's one of the most popular television shows in the nation was the Jerry Springer Show. Although this talk show had been airing since the mid 1980's, it was never popular. Then Jerry Springer changed the format. He started inviting the most crass, ridiculous, and downright offensive people on his show. Rather than being interviewed by Mr. Springer, many times it seemed as if the guests were there just to make a scene and be mocked. Several segments degenerated into outright violence. All the while, the studio audience would be cheering on its feet. Cheering *Jerry Springer*, not the guests. They were not relevant beyond their outrageousness and entertainment value.

This psychology is something Donald Trump obviously understands. But instead of standing off to the side, microphone in hand, with a bemused look on his face, seemingly helpless in the face of others' antics, Trump became the puerile, ridiculous, offensive guest on everyone's nighttime television screens. Trump knows what they want, what works and what doesn't work. And all of America tuned in. Further, Trump was mocking everyone *but* the people sitting at home on the couch that needed replacing years ago. He mocked his former friends. He mocked seasoned politicians and reduced them to school boys. He mocked the moderators supposedly in charge of the whole show. He mocked the very political system that allowed him to become a billionaire multiple times during his seventy years.

"I tell it like it is," Trump said. "She's a fraud", "these guys are on the take" and "Michigan auto workers make too much money".

"I agree with Bernie that we are being ripped off and that HRC has made a fortune off of a lot of people," Trump intimated.

America hung on his every word. He made us believe we could take back control of our country and our lives (jobs that don't pay enough, healthcare that costs too much whether or not one has insurance, higher education that costs more than a starter home but gets you nothing but bills) from the untouchable Washington elite that made things that way and somehow kept getting richer in the process. And he made fools of the political masters who had been fooling us for thirty years.

Only two types of Republican primary voters could resist this appeal: those comfortable enough not to need Trump or his politics (upper middle class, well-educated, well employed, socially liberal [usually]); and principled conservatives - i.e., Middle America

Republicans offended and outraged by Trump's ribald rhetoric ("I just grab them by the ___"), questionable personal morals, bizarre behavior and unprincipled hijacking of our political party, who were unwilling to look beyond the media antics and/or turn down the volume so as not to hear his truly offensive statements in order to capitalise on Trump's power grab. These Republicans were either naive about how corrupt our political system really is or unwilling to take drastic action to change that system - drastic action that might risk losing money, friends or an election. When Donald Trump won the nomination it was too late for these Republicans. There was no longer any effective choice within the Republican party. A new power base had been established. Trump Country.

Cleveland, Ohio
2016 RNC Convention

Ohio was admitted to the union in March 1803. Beginning with the presidential election in November 1804, whichever candidate wins the majority of votes in Ohio has almost always gone on to win the presidency. From 1964 onward the streak has been unbroken. No other state's voters have so consistently chosen the winner. Every time a Republican has won, he has carried Ohio.

I am not going to argue causation here. There is something special about this territory just west of the New York and Pennsylvania borders, with a history that stretches back millenia [sic]. Over 150 years, Yankee and Mid-Atlantic settlers, along with some Southerners from the Upper South, here forged a rooted yet forward-looking culture based on industry in the old sense as well as infrastructure, education and innovation. The Confederation Congress had banned slavery in the Northwest Territory in 1787 before statehood and thus there was no taint to the state's early prosperity. During the

19th century, immigrants from Ireland and Germany often found their way into the Ohio Country, a path which led many to prosper. Ohio was also the way to freedom for many African Americans who escaped slavery and oppression in the south by following the "Underground Railroad" to liberty in Ohio. Many settled there.

Ohio fought with the Union during the Civil War and furnished more than 320,000 troops and countless supplies to the war effort. This was fitting for Ohio's stature at the time, because it was the third most populous state in the union after New York and Virginia.

The next major wave of migrations occurred post World War I, when many Southerners from Appalachia moved north. Many African Americans also moved to Ohio's cities at that time during what is called the "Great Migration." These new populations quickly joined the industrial worker base which made Ohio one of the leading states in arms manufacturing during World War II. During the postwar boom, Ohio's workers grew into the backbone of the American Middle Class. Work in industrial manufacturing, education, advanced technology and other innovating fields lifted many, many families out of poverty and into the mainstream of American life. Ohio was at the forefront.

Ohio was also at the forefront of late Twentieth Century industrial decline. Beginning in the 1970's, jobs and people began to leave Ohio as steel factories and other manufacturing facilities shut down. Ohio was well-served by a state government that pivoted towards medicine, education, and services, and biomedical manufacturing. But these jobs - the good paying ones - were only available for the well-educated. So overall it was a loss.

It also created a wound in the soul of many communities. Since World War II, with the exception of the Vietnam Era, Americans by and large understood that if they worked hard in whatever field they were in and at whatever education level they had attained and obeyed the law, they could get ahead. It might take longer for certain people, but with the successful Civil Rights movement from 1948-1970, the reopening of America to Asian immigration in 1961, and the positive changes these reforms made to American society (equality for everyone and a place in American society for people from all quarters of the globe), everyone could grow. All families could achieve middle class status. The sky was the limit.

With deindustrialization and the shift to the "service economy," the wheels came off. Admittedly, this one factor alone did not tear apart entire communities. Other actions by America's political and economic elite - it is really the same group of people - followed this shift and made its effects worse. Deindustrialization was the first step and the symbolic change that it was no longer important for American men to make things. Somehow that had become "beneath" all of us rather than just the privileged few.

First, good paying manufacturing jobs left town. Union membership decreased. The multi-tiered structure of industrial management collapsed. This structure, which had its origin with the growth of the U.S. military under General George C. Marshall in the 1930's, is sometimes referred to synecdochally as Middle Management. It had turned American society from 1941 to 1970 into a society of leaders. Middle Management permitted the top executives to focus on vision, strategy, and the big picture without getting bogged down by people management issues. Middle Management also provided the volunteer leadership base for the entire country (Boy Scouts, PTA, etc.). With deindustrialization, this collapsed. The great American Middle Class began shrinking and American society began simplifying economically. This was the dawn of the Age of Inequality.

Then, wages at the remaining non-owner operator jobs in town stagnated. According to the Economic Policy Institute (EPI), from 1948 to 1973, the average hourly compensation of Americans in non-management, private sector jobs grew 91.3%. But from 1973 to 2013, average hourly compensation grew only 9.2%. What this means is the average real wage decreased over two generations due to factors outside of the workers' control.

Compare the average wage to top executive compensation. From 1950-1972, CEO compensation averaged being three times that of the average wage. But from 1973-2007, this ballooned to 50:1. Moreover, high executive compensation was combined with a position at all of the tables in the community where decisions are made. This in turn created a new owner class whose members owned and ran everything. Now the PTA and other important community-based nonprofits were run almost exclusively by members and scions of this class, including their spouses. Of this elite, I should say.

Higher education was the one consistent path outward from this dynamic onto more solid financial footing. From 1945-2007, the percentage of Americans with college degrees grew fivefold for men and ninefold for women, which are tremendous accomplishments. On average, an American worker with a college degree will earn around $20,000 more *per year* than a worker who did not successfully pursue higher education. But when we examine the details we can detect the same dynamic of rising costs artificially distributed against working and middle class Americans. From 1963 to 1977, the average cost of tuition at public colleges and universities offering four-year degrees grew 269.5%. But from 1978 - the year of my birth - until 2007, it grew by more than 800%. By comparison, if the federal minimum wage in 1981 ($3.35) grew 800% over the next twenty-six years, the minimum wage in 2007 would have been $26.80 per hour! (In 2020 dollars, that would be $33.50 per hour.)

The actual federal minimum wage in 2007 was $7.25 per hour

Persistently low wages in combination with rising executive compensation, rising higher education costs, and rising home prices acted sclerotically to almost completely block the pipeline into middle class prosperity. What had begun as an aspiration based on a set of civil rights (powers and protections of individuals against government action) in an atmosphere of market-oriented opportunity degenerated into a free-for-all asset grab by the elite. Let's examine one last economic statistic: the networth of federal officials.

While the story did not end there in the late 2000 naughts, the damage had been done and it remains a part of the state's soul. The population has not returned. Starting in 2012, Ohio had only eighteen electoral votes to cast in the presidential election. This is the fewest since 1832, when General Andrew Jackson was elected president.

In 2016 the RNC chose to host its national convention in Ohio. Cleveland, the host city, is the hometown of Lebron James, who led the Cleveland Cavaliers to win the NBA championship that spring. All in all it was a favorable choice.

National political party conventions, which only occur during presidential election years, are the campiest that politics ever becomes, especially once America entered the mass market television era. Before then, conventions were the mechanism for bringing together party leaders and followers from all fifty states. This was the only way it was done at scale. Attendees apparently spend three to four days networking, partying, listening to speeches, and voting. The drinks, stories, celebrities, idols, and women must just flow. It sounds like the ultimate Super Bowl party for political junkies.

In the television era, political party conventions lost both power and magic. Satellite TV, cable, the internet, and social media have conspired to create alternative ways to get one's ideas to thousands of other people. These are ways that do not require getting off the couch, tailor-made for Americans. Further, because rank and file voters are watching, the ability of backroom deals to occur and impact strongly which candidate wins or which issues will be on the ballot has been diminished.

Two highlights have endured: the winner's acceptance speech by the party candidate who has won enough delegates to get on the ballot, and the keynote address.

Ironically, perhaps, the very first keynote address at a Republican National Convention (RNC) was by a Black man. The Honorable John R. Lynch, member of the U.S. House of Representatives for Mississippi's 6th congressional district, gave the keynote address at the 1884 RNC in Chicago, Illinois. He was nominated as Temporary chairman of the convention by a precocious Harvard educated Republican from New York named Theodore Roosevelt.

Usually the keynote is delivered by a state governor or U.S. Senator who may one day run for president themselves. Once every other decade the keynote is given by a U.S. Representative or other federal government official. Rarely is the keynote given by a state level office holder who is not a governor. 2004 proved to be such an occasion for the Democratic party. The keynote was given by an Illinois state senator who was running for the U.S. Senate seat of retiring Senator Peter Fitzgerald.

At the Democratic Party National Convention in 2004, a relatively unknown Illinois State Senator from the Chicago area named Barack Obama gave a speech that changed his career and his country.

What contrast this presents to the 2016 RNC convention speech of candidate Donald Trump.

The Return of Law and Order

Donald Trump launched his convention speech with stinging, evocative rhetoric from the Right: the return of law and order.

In the late 1960's, former California Governor and former Vice President Richard Nixon won a three-way presidential race by promising to restore law and order. During that era, civil rights protests and peace demonstrations had turned American society upside down. Certain Americans stood against the ideals of both of these movements. Other Americans were tired of the upheaval. In came candidate Nixon. Since at the time most Americans (and certainly most Republicans) believed that obeying the law (even racist Jim Crow laws in the southern states the Civil Rights Movement marched against) was a cardinal civic virtue, this appeal was very successful.

Fast forward to 2016. When Donald Trump declared during the first thirty seconds of his acceptance speech, "But we will also be a country of law and order," this certainly made many ears ring.

Among Donald Trump's first promises in his acceptance speech was to restore neighborhood safety and protect the police. Once again, this rhetoric does not contain anything controversial on its face but examined in context, it reveals what some view as a fundamental problem.

Recall that 2015 to 2016 - especially the summers - were bloody years for African Americans. Many were shot and killed during routine traffic stops all over the country. Rarely if it all was there a reasonable ground for the police to pull over these Black motorists. Thankfully, many of these incidents were caught on video through use of smartphones.

This cycle of violence began on June 16, 2015 - the day Donald Trump launched his presidential campaign - when a White teenager walked into a Black church in Charleston, South Carolina on an otherwise normal summer Sunday and proceeded to shoot to death nine parishoners at point blank range. The entire nation was stunned.

On a regular, predictable, and fatal basis, police in America were killing legally innocent, objectively unarmed Black men. And they were being caught on camera. But little justice followed. These White (mostly) men were not removed from office or prosecuted.

As I am writing this book, the cycle of violence continues.

Donald Trump's first message, therefore, was divisive. Many were comforted by his words. Many were outraged.

Candidate Donald Trump continued in the same vein. He asserted very clearly that open borders kill innocent Americans. Then he clearly laid the responsibility for those border policies at the well-shod feet of Senator Hillary Clinton.

Naturally given Donald Trump's demeanor, Hillary Clinton was not his only target. He also set President Barack Obama and his agenda squarely in his gunsites. Under Democrats (Obama) poverty and dependence increase. As Trump put it, "This Administration has failed America's inner cities. It's failed them on education. It's failed them on jobs. It's failed them on crime. It's failed them at every level."

Then Trump launched into his most incendiary statement in the entire speech:

> The irresponsible rhetoric of our President, who has used the pulpit of the presidency to divide us by race and color, has made America a more dangerous environment for everyone.

It is hard to make sense of this statement. I have no idea what rhetoric of Obama's Trump is referring to. More importantly, though, to make such a statement about America's first Black president is a smack in the face. The very election of Barack Hussein Obama was the greatest political triumph of America's better angels over her historic and still-present demons: slavery and willful genocide, racial segregation, antisemitism, misogyny, and economic oppression, despite persistent claims to be a champion of individual liberty and equal justice under law without regard to a person's national origin, sex, religion or way of life. THIS IS WHO WE ARE. And this Donald Trump attacked.

If most Americans who voted in presidential elections actually watched or listened to presidential campaign speeches, for many

Republicans this might have been a dealbreaker. But most of us do not watch the speeches. Or care about them. Therefore, I would bet money that if you had asked the average American who voted for Donald Trump on November 8, 2016, they would have denied that was what he said.Or they would have pointed out how Donald Trump also said: "Anyone who endorses violence, hatred or oppression is not welcome in our country and never will be."

As I move on to other aspects of Candidate Donald Trump's acceptance speech I would like the reader to bear Trump's indictment of Obama on race and division in mind: it will come in handy when analysing President Trump's response to the tragedy in Charlottesville, VA.

The solution to President Obama's policies? Trump promised to repeal and replace "Obamacare" once elected. A straightforward repeal, of course, would entail nullifying the parts of President Obama's healthcare law that are most popular with the middle class among both political parties: prohibiting insurance companies from refusing to provide coverage for adults and children with pre-existing health conditions; eliminating lifetime and annual payout limits; and mandating that insurance companies spend at least 85% of the revenue they receive from premiums on medical coverage or refunding the surplus. Thus "replace" would have to be a central part of Trump's proposal for it to achieve support beyond his base.

Regarding U.S. foreign policy and our reputation among the community of nations, Trump asserted that our reputation has "fallen like the consulate in Bengazi, which was Hillary's fault." According to Trump, on the one hand the U.S. is not respected by the international community the way we deserve. On the other, the U.S. continues to foot the bill for N.A.T.O. and several other international organizations. Trump aims to end this lopsided state of foreign affairs.

One of the Trump campaign's central themes is: *a change in leadership is required to change outcomes.* The politicians who produced this mess won't fix it. In Trump's mind and out of his mouth, those politicians are President Obama, the Clintons and their whole cohort. They and the special interests have rigged the system against the average middle class American worker and his or her family - the nickel-and-dimed normal people who work hard but get nowhere.

The imagery Trump employed in his speech is familiar to anyone who lives in the Rustbelt like I do: shuttered factories and derelict facilities, the byproducts of unfair trade deals. According to Donald Trump, this state of affairs is the fault of Obama and the Clinton machine. The system is rigged. Or as Trump put it, "It was rigged against Bernie Sanders - he never had a chance."

But, Trump promised, he will fix it. "Everyday I wake up determined to deliver for the people who have been neglected, ignored, or abandoned." Indeed, his determination apparently was not the only factor. "Nobody knows the system better than me, which is why I alone can fix it."

According to this acceptance speech, Trump's plan is:

America First. Safety at home, in our neighborhoods, secure borders and protection against terrorism. Restoring law and order; ending domestic Islamic terrorism.

Trump also promised to improve opportunities for children in America's inner cities.

"I am going to bring our jobs back to Ohio and to America." On this point, Candidate Donald Trump had some choice words for the current administration: "This Administration has failed America's inner cities. It's failed them on education. It's failed them on jobs. It's failed them on crime. It's failed them at every level."

Trump declared he would use tariffs against countries that cheat international trade deals.

He said he would oppose bad trade deals and renegotiate others.

Naturally as a businessman and a Republican, Trump proposed a big tax cut. But he also promised to rebuild rotting American infrastructure, free up energy production from regulations, and appoint conservative justices.

In international relations Trump proposed some of the biggest policy shifts. Trump promised to abandon "the failed policy of nation building and regime change [sic]". He also said he would suspend immigration from nations compromised by terrorism and fight illegal immgration from everywhere. For Trump and his supporters, illegal immigration is lawlessness.

Trump's conclusion was one of the stronger parts of his speech, and it contrasted well with the ethos of Senator Hillary Clinton's campaign. In his own words, Trump stated:

> My opponent asks her supporters to recite three-word loyalty pledge. It reads: "I'm With Her". I choose to recite a different pledge. My pledge reads: "I'M WITH YOU – THE AMERICAN PEOPLE." I am your voice. MAGA

If Senator Hillary Rodham Clinton was running for the highest office in the land for anyone, it was not for the people who attended Trump rallies wearing red MAGA hats. It was not for the chronically unemployed men in shuttered factory towns. It was not for the hard-working socially conservative middle class types who questioned why their employer-provided health insurance plan's premiums keep going up by double-digit percentages each year for the exact same services by the exact same doctors and nurses. Nor was it for the middle class African Americans fed up with the endemic corruption and perpetual mismanagement of Chicago, Detroit, Baltimore, Atlanta, and other Democrat-run "Black" cities. All of these persons desperately wanted change, and they knew for certain it would never come on Senator Clinton's watch.

Somehow a brash braggart billionaire from N.Y. with funny hair and a potty mouth managed to communicate to people who will never stay at Mar-a-lago that he would fight for them. And on November 8, they voted for him.

Overall this speech, which without a doubt was watched by more Americans than Trump's first campaign speech, was mediocre. Trump announced little that was new. He had already announced in other fora his plan for the agenda of his administration and the direction in which he wished to take our country. Trump said little about how his family background and business experience as N.Y. real estate industry leader made him a strong candidate for the presidency. On the other hand, his sloppy rhetoric and tone-deaf attitude - apparent throughout much of the speech - made him more enemies than necessary.

At bottom, I don't think Trump's acceptance speech won him any votes he did not already have whereas the speech that launched his presidential run helped win him the office.

I wish to analyze one last speech of Trump's first campaign before moving onto what Donald Trump accomplished during his first term in office and what he failed at.

The speech was not one of the barnstorm Trump Rally speeches. This one was a policy speech focused on immigration reform, made in the conservative border state of Arizona on August 31, 2016.

Trump established the tone of his speech during the opening two minutes. He was going to discuss in detail his views on immigration, why he has them, and what he intends to do to fix America's immigration problem. At the core was the cardinal Trumpian principle of America First. Or in this instance, Americans First - Americans over illegal aliens; American workers over foreign workers; the American Constitution and federal laws over executive orders granting amnesty and protections to persons in the U.S. illegally.

Trump promised ten specific actions to reverse the status quo on illegal aliens and amnesty:

- Build the wall
- End the catch and release policy by deporting directly those caught crossing the border illegally
- Locate and deport quickly all criminal illegal aliens
- Block funding for sanctuary cities
- Enforce all immigration laws
- Suspend offering visas to citizens of places that cannot provide adequate security screening
- Ensure that the countries of origin for deported persons take them back
- Create a biometric entry visa tracking system [sic]

- Prevent foreigners from obtaining jobs and benefits
- Reform immigration laws to benefit Americans.

Being a big salesman, Candidate Trump included a sales hook designed to motivate voters to support his agenda:

> "This election is our last chance to secure the border, stop illegal immigration, and reform our laws to make your life better. This is it. We won't get another opportunity – it will be too late."

It was not the type of speech Trump's liberal critics would have expected. Nor would they have given him credit for detailed policy analysis. To them the Donald was a crass, womanizing racist. There was no complexity and no intellect, let alone depth. Once again these critics were blind to the power of Donald Trump to pick an issue many Americans care about, state his disrupting viewpoint and articulate a rationale that would sell beyond Trump's base.

This explains the shock in the early morning on November 9th. It did not occur to the intellectuals on the Left that there was a coherent message from Donald Trump on specific policy points that actually mattered to normal Americans, let alone one that could achieve widespread appeal with the electorate.

But it does not explain the rage. The only idea I can come up with to explain the Left's rage against Donald Trump and his voters is entitlement. They believe they can tell us how things ought to be. They believe they are the only ones qualified to lead. They do not care about the feelings or circumstances of individuals beyond their exalted circles, although they do care about groups outside of their circles. Thus the plumbers' union local number whatever and its leaders matter more than the individuals who actually pay the dues.

The problem in November 2016 for liberals was that after twenty-one years of NAFTA, the plumbers got the message and voted for someone who would fight for their interests.

PART III

ELECTION NIGHT IN AMERICA

$\cdots\cdots\bullet\bullet\bullet\bullet\bullet\bullet\bullet\bullet\bullet\bullet\bullet\bullet\bullet\cdots$

Other than Superbowl Sunday, more Americans sit around the television after 9 P.M. on election night than any other night. The drama, the history, the power, the surprises of unforeseen upsets or come-from-behind victories - election night has it all. And at this point in our national story, every American adult who is not a felon has an unalienable right to participate in this national drama. An equal right. Every vote counts.

For candidates, though, the experience of election night transcends passive entertainment. Our futures are at stake. Most likely our bank accounts were drained by the effort to achieve a victory that remains uncertain. Not only that, our identities, our sense of who we are as politicians and why we exist is put to trial on Election Day as at no other time. Regardless of the outcome, we have participated in something great. We have been initiated into a quasi-sacred rite of priesthood in our national civic religion.

Defeat crushes. Some candidates never recover. Other candidates seem to take it in stride, knowing that because we are a democracy, so long as the earth and the U.S. Constitution endure, there will always come another Election Night.

Victory is glorious! You are lauded, loved and worshipped by masses of people completely ignorant of your inner thoughts, emotions and motivations. They love you! Henceforth, you shall walk and act like a king. For a brief moment you have become like a god. You may do whatever you please, unassailable.

Fools! Fools and puppets, all. As if man were more than dust, and the True God would not demand a higher reckoning.

There is another side to victory as well. Once you win, the enemies you have made through your campaign become permanent. For there is no one who can run for office without making enemies. Spit in your face during an argument; a door slammed on your nose in mid sentence; outstretched hand left unshaken; physical assaults; property destruction; slights to your family; threatened job loss; sinister predictions. All of these things happen regularly on the campaign trail.

But a candidate who loses is easy to forgive. Not only did he or she prove to be harmless but now they look ridiculous, a broke laughing stock, a clown with the paint off but still in baggy pants and oversize shoes. What is the effect when you run into him in the local grocery store? What is it like working in the cubical across from her at her mid level job? Awkward, but harmless.

Victors are not forgiven by their enemies because in politics the victors possess the one thing their enemies fear - legitimate power. Now the man or woman whom you don't like and whose family you won't associate with has the legitimate power to carry out the agenda you despise, upend your life and make the future difficult for your kids and grandkids, and there ain't a darn thing you can do about it.

So the plotting continues. It also shifts gears, becomes organized, incorporates, raises funds, recruits soldiers. Their new mission is to bring you down by any means necessary.

If your enemies include persons who also hold political office (and they almost certainly will), then you should expect more than mere character assassination in the local press (protected by the First Amendment as the quintessential right of political speech) and minute, merciless scrutiny of every word you speak and each decision you make. You should expect calls for public inquiry. You should expect public bodies to form committees to investigate allegations of your wrongdoing. You should expect calls for you to testify to explain yourself to persons who purport to sit in judgment over you even though they were not elected to do so. You should expect these committees (who always seem to contain the same persons) to conclude their business by issuing an inconclusive report calling for further investigation. You should expect to pay for all of this out of your tax dollars.

You should expect all of this beginning on Election Night, for this is how the species of humanity called American does politics.

I know all of this, because I am a politician. I have run in two election campaigns thus far, both of which were fought in upstate New York. I am a Republican.

For those not familiar with the geographic and historical divide that created and sustains upstate New York as a place and upstate New Yorkers as a people, New York State was settled east of the Hudson River by the Dutch. From Albany downward to Manhattan and eastward to Nassau County, Long Island, the cultural landscape still bears the imprint of those enterprising traders who embraced diversity centuries ago, but who also tolerated vast inequities of property. In other words, massive fortunes and slavery would be protected, but so would religious and a surprising amount of racial diversity. Not that everyone enjoyed the political franchise but individuals were certainly freer than in the English colonies that mostly surrounded "New Amsterdam" and "New Holland." While the English took control of this colony in 1667 and renamed it New York after James Stuart, the Duke of York, brother of the king of Great Britain, the founder DNA of the Dutch - their names, ethos and way of commerce and life - continued to predominate.

However when one moves westward and crosses the Hudson River, one enters a different country. This region is mostly rural - farms and forest, with countless small towns scattered throughout. It is watered by two of the largest freshwater lakes in the world and a family of smaller "Finger Lakes"; long fertile valleys were carved by the mighty Mohawk River flowing eastward, the mighty Susquehanna River flowing southward, and the mighty Genesee River flowing northward. The bookends are two formerly great American industrial powerhouses - Buffalo and Rochester. Upstate New York, as this province is named, provides homes and a different way of life for approximately 6.5 million people living mostly in small cities and towns.

Upstate, the founder DNA has two branches: Yankees descended from English and Welsh colonists in Massachusetts and Connecticut largely settled upstate and brought their missional, small town, local democracy and public education mindset, and their notions of respectable (meaning non-ostentatious) affluence. Meanwhile, along the 283 mile southern border of the state and inland for about fifty miles, another culture settled down. Its roots began in upcountry Pennsylvania, South Carolina, and Georgia, where life and work were less industrial and more down to earth. The people were friendly at a distance but very clannish, armed to the teeth and vigilant about their rights. Land and freedom were their all. Think Braveheart. Seriously.

The Appalachian Mountain chain served as the internal highway for this culture. Movement was always in two directions: northeastward or southwestard. The top end of this mountain chain juts abruptly into Upstate New York, and so did this culture. It is part of the bedrock.

These founder DNA "tribes" were supplemented for generations by millions of Irish, Italian, Polish, Slovak, Ukrainian, and other European immigrants. Many found work in factories throughout the upstate urban landscape for generations before the shifting of that commerce destroyed a way of life. The children moved onward to the West or to the South. Yet a vibrant cultural core remains.

During the last eighty years, these populations were further supplemented by a million African Americans who either migrated directly from the Old South to upstate New York or who more often came upstate via New York City. Sometimes, these families stopped off in the City for a generation or two, before heading upstate where the air is cleaner, the people friendlier, the way of life easier. We remain here at levels that are politically and culturally significant.

I was born and bred upstate in the Genesee Country around Rochester, New York, Frederick Douglass's town. My family has lived there since the 1950's. Both branches came via New York City and moved westward quickly. My father, Dorollo Nixon, was born in segregated North Carolina in a county with an almost even racial balance of Black and White. In the mid fifties, his mother moved him and two siblings to Queens, New York, before quickly settling on Long Island, where my dad would wrestle in high school.

But his life (and through him those of his children and grandchildren) was transformed when he moved upstate to pursue a bachelor's degree. He moved from a poor, overcrowded, racially segregated hamlet in West Hempstead, Long Island, 430 miles northwestward into a racially integrated state university dorm in a small village bisected by the Erie Canal. One would be hard pressed to invent a greater contrast within New York State that would involve large amounts of people.

Dad had found a place where he was supported in pursuing his dreams, where he found meaningful and challenging work in public education and where he faced little racial discrimination. He never returned downstate.

My parents met at college in that small canal village. My mother's father, the Reverend Randle Edward Witcher, Sr., was a Pentecostal pastor who moved from Virginia to New York City twice during the 1940's. The moves bookended his military service during World War II, alongside hundreds of thousands of other African Americans. In the late 1950's, my grandpa's denomination sent him, along with my grandma and six of what would eventually be eight children, to pastor a small congregation upstate in Rochester, New York. The church was in the nineteenth ward, which was or quickly became the area of greatest Black population density between Buffalo and New York City - almost 500 miles. My grandpa settled and remained in the Rochester area for the next thirty years. He lived to see most of his children settle prosperously there and to hold more than a dozen grandchildren. My grandma, who survived him by twenty years, lived to hold their great-great grandchildren.

In this blessed and beautiful country it is natural for me to be a Republican. I prize individual freedom; I accept the necessity of individual responsibility as an indivisible part of freedom. I value higher education and hold two degrees; by God's grace I have prospered. I revere the U.S. Constitution and respect our laws. The law has not hurt me arbitrarily. Moreover, I desire to see more individuals enjoying liberty and its fruits. Thus I favor large amounts of immigration to our country without quotas or skill requirements, for that is what built up our great nation.

These are my politics.

From this core I derive my policy preferences: a strong national defense balanced with diplomatic engagement as well as budget responsibility; flat taxes, because they are fair; no abortion, because it's murder; robust but temporary social welfare benefits - "it's a safety net, not a safety lifestyle" ; broad access to higher education through government backed loans; support for traditional American folk life and religion - "Merry Chistmas" not "Happy Holidays"; Christmas decorations and messages on public property unless the public votes not to; prayers before civic events if the civic body so desires.

In my view and in my families' experiences, the surest way out of poverty and into opportunity is through higher education.

As I said earlier, I am a politician. I have run for office twice: the 2012 Republican Primary in New York Congressional District 29 (which no longer exists) and the 2016 State Assembly Election in Assembly District 123 (which soon will no longer look the way it does now). I dropped out of the first race when a path to victory no longer seemed viable. It was not the money; it was the balloting, a creature of insider politics albeit a necessary one in my opinion. The second race I ran until the end - Election Night 2016.

There is no room for private drama on election night, especially for candidates. First, no candidate spends election night on the couch surrounded by friends and family. You are running for a public office. You spend Election Night in a public place, preferably one that serves alcohol. You might need it.

Second, despite the fact that only one person's name goes on the ballot, campaigning is a team sport. Thus the candidate will not be alone in a crowded public space; the whole team will be there - communications, advance, advisors, the treasurer, the chief of staff, assorted handlers. Everyone is ready to watch the future unfold. Their future.

Third, candidates don't stand alone on a platform. They belong to a political party. That party at the county level, its smallest unit of organic integrity, will have rented an ample space to hold its own victory party. Praises will ring out to the rafters. Lybations will flow. Tables placed conveniently away from the dozen or so TV screens will groan with catered spreads. As a candidate you have an automatic invite. So does your team. (You don't want to pay for your own booze, do you?) But don't go too early. You would not want to appear like an unweaned step child.

That's the social architecture. Now onto the process. It is two-fold: watching results and talking to friends, supporters, strangers. That's it. Nothing hi-tech. No secret wizardry. Just eat a finger sandwich, take a sip, and speak pleasantries to your neighbor all the while keeping a discrete eye on the nearest television.

Periodically your conversations will be interrupted by chairs as the media reports estimated vote counts and percentages, which the audience greets with cheers. You take it all in stride. After all, you just ate catered food that cost you nothing.

Eat, drink and wait. I spent Election Night 2016 in my friends' bar, aptly named The Colonial. The team was there. Friends stopped by to say hello, shake a hand, trying to appropriate some of that glory that would have been mine if I had won. Everyone wishes you luck.

The night for me was disappointing. My numbers never really got there to be competitive against a fourteen-year incumbent in a small community. I tried to maintain perspective. Interestingly, no one offers to buy me a drink. People want to drink with winners. I tried not to think of the shambles of campaign finance, how little was left in the bank.

Fatefully, the news from the presidential race began to intrude on my thoughts. Something extraordinary was taking place. I began to lose focus on my election results and focus on the presidency. Was it possible that history was being made tonight?

Donald Trump was winning. By a lot. All over the country. And it wasn't even 9 P.M.! Giddy with excitement like children on a train headed for the North Pole, we could hardly believe we were on our way to meet the big fat old white man.

By 8:30 P.M. our eyes had turned irresistibly to the televisions. Trump had already won several states - including some "fly over states" which many liberals openly disdain. In California and along the west coast the polls weren't even closed yet. But, no Republican since Ronald Reagan has won California in the presidency and no Republican candidate worth his weight in judgment would count on the Golden State in order to win.

The states we focused on were Florida, Pennsylvania, Virginia, Ohio, and Wisconsin. If Donald Trump won four of the five of these states and the balance of the election played out along party lines, he would win the presidency.

It seemed almost impossible to believe. The crass braggart and foul-mouthed real estate and media billionaire might actually get elected president. He might actually become the most powerful man in the world. At that point, would his ambitions admit to any impediments? Moreover, he would get elected as a Republican? He was married three times! But he was chosen by the party of the "Moral Majority." He had obviously had a host of other women. Yet many Republican men attended and spoke highly of the "Promise Keepers" movement whose evangelical goals include strengthening men's commitments in our relationships as husbands and fathers. The man with the orange hair who had made his reputation and first fortune by promoting gambling? Many Republicans view gambling as a sin. So how was it possible?

God knows. No. Seriously.

That was not an attempt to avoid explaining or justifying why I and many others like me voted for a man whose character we find objectively execrable and whose businesses we would not patronize. The reasons were complex, and I will explore them a little later.

8:45 P.M. - Ohio and Florida are definitely in play. We felt a buzz of excitement moving around the bar. Many of us knew what that meant and for the others, no doubt the commentators on every channel were telling them - no Republican presidential candidate has ever won without winning Ohio. Ohio is a must win, or this is not the United States of America.

Trump won Ohio.

All eyes turn to Florida. Florida, that once sleepy state whose northern third is more southern than Georgia. Florida, with its millions of retired Northerners. Florida, with its sizeable Jewish population - the second largest in the entire nation. Florida, whose southern tip is more Hispanic than Texas. Florida, whose coastal islands are either ultra-rich enclaves or forgotten backwaters. Florida transformed herself from worm to monarch butterfly at the beginning of this century.

Florida was the third state of the Bushes (after Connecticut and Texas), the family that remade the GOP post-Reagan. Florida was crucial in the 2000 Presidential election win of George W. Bush. And voting problems in Florida, then governed by his brother Jeb Bush, and Supreme Court intervention, handed George Bush the victory. But that was not the end of Florida's time in the sunshine.

Florida's electoral power has grown with its population. That is natural for any democracy. But it is the swift rise in Florida's population that is noteworthy. In 1980, Florida had less than ten million residents. By 2000, the year of the contested presidential election in which Florida, governed by Jeb Bush, played a central role, the population had increased 63% to more than sixteen million. By the end of 2014, Florida's population had grown to almost twenty million residents, and the Sunshine State overtook New York as the third most populous state in our nation. This swift rise is the foundation of Florida's continuing electoral power.

For the sake of comparison, let us also examine Illinois, the state and power base of President Barack Obama. In 1960, Illinois had a population of more than ten million residents - a *greater* population than Florida had twenty years later. But Illinois' net population peaked "demographically" around 1970. What I mean by that term is that an analysis of Illinois' population growth alongside its birth rate shows that more adults left the state than remained in the state even though the net population grew. Only adults vote. Thus births, which count as population, are not as impactful politically as a family choosing to relocate to another state. Five births minus one family of four leaving the state equals a net statistical growth of one person. But politically, it equals a loss many times greater.

In 1970, Illinois' population was 11,110,285. It would take *more than a quarter century* for the population to go up by one million souls. Despite more than two decades elapsing since Illinois reached a population of twelve million, Illinois has never broken through the barrier to thirteen million.

All the while, Illinois has been home to Chicago, our nation's third largest city and still one of our great metropolises.

Here is a twenty year snapshot of the most important statistics that support these measurements. All statistics below are from the Illinois Department of Public Health unless otherwise indicated.

Between 1990 and 2009, there were 3,674,692 live births in Illinois. During the same time period, there were 2,084,223 deaths of Illinois residents. The gain by births over deaths is 1,590,469.

Between July 1991 and July 2009, Illinois' population grew by 1,367,610.

The difference between these two measures through 2009 represents the outmigration of adults and their families. In Illinois' case, 222,859 residents over approximately twenty years.

Only adults vote. Only adults choose to move. Thus the political consequences of Illinois' demographic issues are staggering. Most of the persons who died in Illinois during that twenty year span were adults, thankfully. Let us assume that 75% of the deaths that occurred during those nineteen years were of adults, 90% of whom were eligible to vote. Let us further assume that half of the Illinois residents who moved out of the state between 1990 and 2009 were children when they left and remain children for the purposes of this calculation. The result shows that Illinois lost more than one million voters during twenty years. This is almost a tenth of the state's average annual population during those years.

I do not know how many of those Illinois voters moved to Florida. But obviously demographic disasters like New York and Illinois contribute to the electoral power of Florida.

U.S. Senator Marco Rubio, the son of Cuban immigrants, is a native Floridian and a rising start in both the Senate and in the GOP. Senator Rubio and his beautiful family - one wife, a former Miami Dolphins cheerleader, and four children all under 18 - represents the future of how the GOP can grow. A future that is young, brown, inclusive but staunchly American. One with a strong military challenging the world's bullies and engaged in ending the world's conflicts, a strong foreign policy, domestic prosperity, open to immigration and to new ideas. In other words, much of what Donald Trump appeared to stand against. Senator Rubio was one of the last candidates to drop out of the 2016 presidential race.

Florida also grew in cultural power from 2000 onward. Tiger Woods famously lives on an island in Palm County, Florida, and took the entire golf world by storm, winning fourteen majors faster than any player ever. During the twenty-first century, Florida hosted the Super Bowl five times before the 2016 presidential cycle - 2001, 2005, 2007, 2009, and 2010. Florida hosted the 2012 RNC Convention. The Miami Heat won the NBA championship three times this century, including in 2016. And a Florida team even managed to win the Stanley Cup: the Tampa Bay Lightning won the cup in 2004.

There is a mystique to Florida. Somehow she radiates sunshine and strength, opportunity and diversity all at the same time. Florida is a twenty-first century state, a place to which more Americans relocate to pursue their dreams than almost any other state. And the people stay. Florida is to this century what Ohio was to the nineteenth century and California to the twentieth century - the land of American opportunity.

And by nine o'clock on Election Night, Trump was winning Florida. He was winning America.

Let us cover two technicalities that could trip people up in their analyses of why Donald Trump won the first time. First, the popular vote count shows Senator Hillary Rodham Clinton won the popular vote. But every high school civic student who passes the course knows that you win the presidency by garnering the most votes in the Electoral College. As a result, winning the popular vote holds no legal or constitutional significance. Despite how loudly Democrats beat the drum, winning the popular vote does not win a candidate the highest office in the land.

Not that Democrats should complain. In 1960, the young U.S. Senator from Massachusetts, John Fitzgerald Kennedy, lost the popular vote to the also young sitting Vice President Richard Milhaus Nixon of California. They did not complain then. In 2000 and 2016, when the phenomenon reoccurred with the popular vote, the Electoral College winner was a Republican.

You may ask, "Is that fair?" Fair has nothing to do with it. The Framers did not design the Electoral College to be either fair or democratic. They designed it specifically to impede democratic power. As Alexander Hamilton stated in the Federal Papers, the device was designed as a failsafe to protect against the voters choosing a candidate who is too dangerous, unstable or otherwise unfit for the presidency. Back then they could write like this without even a hint of irony. Back then they did not even need to concern themselves with the madness of King George.

Second, states are not blank slates political, against which electoral battles play out. Rather, states have history, character, demographic and socio-economic patterns - all of which change slowly. A majority of voters in most states consistently choose only one party's candidate. Thus before Election Night, politicians, historians, economists, and others who pay attention to what happens in the political arena know with great certainty which states each presidential candidate is likely to win.

However, there are a handful of states that can go either way - the swing states. The entire Electoral College winning process depends on winning enough votes from swing states. Further, given the demographic shifts that occur within our nation during the ten years between U.S. censuses - a well-established pattern throughout much of our nation's history - the particular swing states a candidate needs to win will shift on a case by case basis.

In 2016, Donald Trump had to win Pennsylvania, Wisconsin, and Michigan. If he did that, and the rest of the states fell into their foreknown pattern, he would win the presidency.

Pennsylvania politically is a blue coast alongside the Delaware and Schuylkill Rivers, centered around Philadelphia, and two inland blue dots. These areas are surrounded by a mass of upland red. More than half of Pennsylvania is part of the Appalachian Mountain chain, and if you believe NPR, more than half of the upcountry mentality is suitably Appalachian. This makes the mentality similar to that of the Southern Tier of New York, where I live. In fact, the border area is affectionately referred to as the Twin Tiers.

Pennsylvania politically holds a special place in my memory. Early in the morning on November 5, 2008, after returning from a run in the deserts of Dubai, where I was then living, I received a call from America on my cell phone. It was Eugene, one of my best friends, calling to let me know Senator Barack Obama had won the presidency. We were elated.

What I also remember about the phone call, though, were the noises in the background: screaming, fireworks, police sirens, perhaps even singing. Thousands upon thousands raised their voices in the streets of America's second capital city in joyful crescendo. The residents of Philadelphia, the City of Brotherly Love, who are mostly Black, were celebrating this historic victory.

By 9:30 P.M. on Election Night 2016, Donald Trump was winning Pennsylvania.

Admittedly I know much less about Michigan and only a few things about the Badger State so I will discuss Michigan.

Another of my best friends grew up in Michigan. We vacationed there together once in the early Naughts. It was lovely.

When I think of Michigan, I think of football before politics. I also think of Detroit and its decayed cultural and political power. But we still hear the echoes of its glory. The Detroit Red Wings won the Stanley Cup twice during the twenty-first century in 2002 and

2008. The Detroit Tigers made it to the World Series in both 2006 and 2012, although victory eluded them.

Detroit was having a rough few decades. In 1990, more than one million people called Detroit home. By 2015, that figure had dropped to 679,305, a loss of approximately one-third. Much of the city's infrastructure was in shambles, and several neighborhoods appeared abandoned.There is more to Michigan than Detroit. Much more, especially politically.

Of Michigan's approximately 9,932,000 residents (according to 2015 data), more than 9,252,000 lived outside of Detroit. The population of Michigan as a whole increased during that time frame by around 6%.

Donald Trump only won Michigan by around 10,704 votes. Did these demographic factors help him win? Maybe. But in my opinion the false assumption of Senator Hillary Clinton that she did not need to campaign much in Michigan did more damage than can be shown by demographic statistics. After all, Michigan is a swing state and it had sixteen electoral votes in 2016. Nevada, by contrast, had only six. Senator Clinton went to Nevada at least four times in 2016, as late as November 2, 2016 - the week before the election - and spent a total of six days in the state since winning the Democratic party nomination in early June 2016. In contrast, she spent only four days in Michigan, which had ten *more* electoral votes.

Senator Clinton spent zero days in Wisconsin from Nomination Night (June 7, 2016) through Election Night. According to Ballotpedia, she lost Wisconsin by 22,748 votes. It had ten electoral votes in 2016.

I went home around 10 P.M. on Election Night, after a painful stop over at our county GOP victory party. My assembly race was one of the biggest electoral races in our county that year, and I lost. But as I headed home I was certain Donald Trump would win the presidency, and so were millions of other Americans.

In terms of strategy, despite the above referenced errors, Senator Clinton's strategy was basically sound and she outraised Donald Trump by hundreds of millions of dollars. That rarely happens. Money does not explain why she lost.

What was more impactful, in my view, was the Walmart Effect.

The Walmart Effect

Sam Walton bought a variety store in Newport, Arkansas, in 1945, before he had even turned thirty years old. He was a typical American man of his generation: unknown but ambitious. But Sam Walton was atypical in that he possessed a willingness to look at common things differently.

Walton looked differently at three aspects of business: how retail goods were sourced, how retail goods were priced, and how a company's employees were treated. Sam Walton's innovations to all three placed him and his family among the top ten richest people on earth for decades.

To source goods for his stores, Walton upended the orthodoxy of arbitrage. Accepted business practice was (and is) to buy low and sell high; the differential minus your costs equals your profit. Then you repeat. If you lower your price, you will probably increase revenue, because who doesn't love a sale? But, your profit margin will be lower, so you will end up with less money.

Walton sourced his goods by searching for below bargain offers: whatever was cheapest and as much as he could get. This included going directly to wholesalers and distributors. Then he sold the goods ... for dirt cheap prices. What he discovered was that even though he would lose some profit on each individual sale, he sold multiple times the number of goods, yielding greater overall profits. This in turn led to two new challenges: how to keep enough goods in stock when customers won't stop buying them; and how to find more customers to absorb his goods. This brings us to the next element of the Walmart Effect: location.

Sam Walton intentionally chose locations for his Walmart stores that were rural or in small towns, underserved and/or growing. He shunned urban areas. In this way he went where others did not and quickly established local market dominance. Further, he went where the future was developing while others lagged behind or did not see the pattern of change at all.

Critically, from Sam Walton's point of view, the challenge was never how to get more customers. An abundance of customers was always waiting just over the hill and around the bend - too far from traditional urban based retailers for them to see or to care. Further, Walton was always committed to the future, committed to where and how things would grow.

In his first fifteen years in business as a retailer, Sam Walton built fifteen variety stores. Approximately two decades later when he launched Walmart he was no longer an unknown. K-mart, one of the nation's leading retailers, was aware that Sam Walton from Arkansas was making paradigm-shifting innovations.

Not that this knowledge did any good for the competition. The problem with Walton's bigger, more established rivals, was just that - they were bigger and more established. This inevitably led management to become complacent with the status quo of how business was done and arrogant about their particular companies' ability to fight off competition.

Today Walmart is the biggest retailer on earth, generating almost half a trillion dollars in revenue per year. K-mart, J.C. Penney's (Sam Walton's first employer), Woolworths (founded in 1879 in Utica, N.Y.; publically traded on the New York Stock Exchange from 1912-1997; a component of the Dow Jones Industrial Average from 1924-1997), and Sears Roebuck & Co. are now all bankrupt or defunct.

How does this apply to the 2016 presidential election? First, Donald Trump's campaign strategy incorporated enough of Sam Walton's retail strategy to achieve its own Walmart Effect. Trump held campaign rallies in smaller cities or towns that traditional candidates ignored or shunned. This allowed him to reach voters who were out of the way and underserved. These voters were far from complacent or comfortable. They had real gripes about the status quo of American business, politics and life, and they desperately wanted change. On November 8, 2016, they voted for Donald Trump.

Second, if one were to look at a national map of Walmart locations, pretty much everywhere there is a store, that county voted for Donald Trump. While this last assertion has some exceptions (e.g., Monroe County, N.Y., where I was born, has seven Walmarts and voted for Senator Clinton), it creates a picture of the base of support for the Trump presidency. Just like Walmart Supercenters are located throughout our country so are Donald Trump's supporters.

If I wanted to tweak that statistic to make it more accurate I would state it this way: every county in America that has three Walmarts or less and has less than 500,000 people voted for Donald Trump. While several million urbanites living across the country voted for Trump, his appeal to them was not compelling. They did not need him to win. The small town dwellers who remained after the boom left, the laid off factory workers now earning hourly wages with no benefits, the small business owners struggling to manage rising minimum wages, the people for whom the American dream vanished in the night during the 1990's - these people voted for Trump in droves, because they needed him to change America for the better.

Another way of capturing this effect is to tally the total number of counties Donald Trump won on Election Night. While the AP and Time magazine, who both reported on this issue, count counties differently, based on either calculation Donald Trump won more votes in more than 83% of the counties in America.

Why is that significant? The county represents the intersection of regional government and local society. With few exceptions, counties bring together a number of different, sometimes rival, municipalities containing different natural features and industries. The county is the most basic attempt to provide uniform governance to diverse people and circumstances. Counties often tax real estate ownership and the sale of goods. Counties also undertake road, bridge and highway construction and repair. Socially, counties are small places. Local society, with its stars and scandals, dirt and drama, holds center stage. On the county level, it matters where you went to high school, even if you became a doctor.

The fact that Donald Trump won the popular vote in more than 80% of America's counties is the greatest non-legal measurement of the legitimacy of his victory. While it may not mean that more Americans voted for Trump, it does mean that more Americans in more places voted for Trump than for Clinton.

Finally, a note on the popular vote. Senator Hillary Clinton received approximately 2.87 million more votes on Election Night than Donald Trump did. But she lost. Due to the structure and function of the Electoral College, Donald Trump received seventy-seven more electoral votes than Senator Clinton did, winning 304 electoral votes. 270 were needed for victory, so Trump still had room to manoeuvre.

These statistics are not news, which is to say that they do not give us new information about the election or the election process; the use of electoral votes to choose the President of the United States is well-known and increasingly unpopular [sic] on the Left. Some view the Constitutional procedure of the Electoral College as patently unfair. Why shouldn't the winner of the popular vote be entitled to win the presidency? Perhaps we should dispense with the Electoral College and go to a straight popular vote?

Rather than respond to this recurring, partisan, circular argument, I want to point to a statistic that is news, or at least was to me. In N.Y.C, Senator Hillary Clinton received more than 2 million more popular votes than Trump, and on top of that she only carried four of N.Y.C's five counties. If the arguments against the Electoral College were accepted and it were abolished, then one city of 319 square miles would decide the fate of a country of more than 3.9 million square miles.

Does that seem fair?

Donald Trump won because most voters in most counties in America voted for him. This may not be the legal or political reason that he won, but it is the spiritual reason he won. His appeal went straight to the heart of most of America, geographically and culturally. That would be difficult to achieve for a bi-coastal elitist or a creature that crawled out of the D.C. Swamp. These points will be important to remember when we examine the reasons Donald Trump will win again in 2020.

Before we move on to analyze Trump's first administration, I would like to take a look at some individuals and groups who voted for Trump, to the shock of the Left.

Black, Hispanic, and Asian Voters

According to CNN exit poll data, 28% of Hispanics voted for Donald Trump. According to exit poll data from Edison Research, it was 29%. Candidate Donald Trump made a host of scathing remarks about Mexicans during his first presidential campaign, and that is putting it mildly. Middle America was shocked, no doubt, to listen to a candidate running in 2016 call a different nationality a bunch of rapists and killers. You figure this type of far-right, anachronistic rhetoric would have caused them to switch off the television and vote for HRC.

Wrong.

Now I know we Republicans (especially moderates) invented a thousand and one excuses to explain away Trump's racist rhetoric. Not very convincingly either.

But the fact that more than a quarter of Hispanic voters voted for Trump is truly shocking.

Why did they do it? First of all, I admit that I am not a Hispanic Black - like a Black Cuban American or a Dominican or a man from Belize. So I am speaking about another ethnic group's thoughts and feelings almost out of vacuum. But I have lived with, worked with, partied with and loved Hispanics or Latinos during adulthood. This gives perspective, and it also creates a willingness to give them the benefit of the doubt.

So why did 28 or 29% of Hispanic voters pull for Donald J Trump? I believe there are three factors. First, Hispanics and Latinos are not a monolith, just like Black people are not a monolith. Blacks have different backgrounds and experiences under the common heading of a skin color that, frankly, does not accurately describe how we think or look. But it does describe how we are treated at its worst. This common bond of race among Black Americans, though, is mostly positive. The heritage and legacy of struggle and survival, fighting and prevailing, marching and persuading hostile neighbors to treat us as men and as women deserve to be treated took place against some of the worst odds in history that a folk who passionately desire to be free have ever faced. To our credit, we have achieved seemingly earth-shattering triumphs like winning gold and flaunting it in Adolph Hitler's face in the 1936 Olympics in Berlin, to organizing a law firm that systematically demolished almost seventy years of racist legislation in the courtroom, to electing a Black American to the highest office in the land in a country where 70% of people were White. We have also struggled persistently and publicly to do basic things our neighbors of other races and backgrounds take for granted, like completing high school and avoiding illegal drugs and teen pregnancies.

Moreover, because we are not a monolith, the triumphs and struggles have not played out evenly (dare I say equally?). The Black lawyer facing racism in the boardroom and fighting back does not face the same circumstances as the Black teen male unjustly arrested in his poor inner city neighborhood by a White male policeman because the policeman planted evidence. It is not the same experience. They do not possess the same resources. It is naive to maintain that all racism is the same.

While for several reasons it is not popular to admit it, the Black experience is shaped by factors like class, education and geographic location. I was born in the late 1970's in the North. There were fundamental differences growing up in the 1980's and early 1990's in an upper middle class suburban housing tract in western New York where three families out of twenty-eight were Black, than there was growing up in a similar class setting outside of Houston, Texas - a place where the entire subdivisions are Black. Schooling, playing, sports, and dating were all the same activities but the different ways those experiences unfolded were like night and day. Sometimes, it did not feel like the same country.

Back to Hispanics: they are not a monolith either, but even more so than Blacks, because people of different races in a race-mad country are all Hispanics, because of a shared linguistic background and/or national origin. There are Hispanics who don't speak Spanish, just as there are Chinese Americans who did not grow up speaking Chinese. From my point of view as an outsider, Hispanics seem very national-origin conscious, especially when it comes to politics. Thus there are as many Puerto Rican Democrats, like Congresswoman Alexandra Ocasio-Cortez of New York, as there are Cuban American Republicans, like U.S. Senator Marco Rubio of Florida.

Further, there is a geographic aspect to Hispanic identity that fundamentally shapes the thoughts and behaviors of Hispanic Americans, in my opinion. The two politicians mentioned above come from and live in East Coast communities of relatively recent origin. Cuban immigrants began settling in southern Florida (especially in Dade County) in the late 1950's, simultaneously with the civil unrest and socialist revolution in Cuba. The Puerto Rican community in N.Y.C is very numerous today, numbering around 800,000 residents. However, if one backs up a hundred years, there were only 7,364 Puerto Ricans living in N.Y.C.

What would make a Hispanic vote for Donald Trump? Simply posing the question is almost an insult. Are not Hispanics men and women like the rest of us? Are they not entitled, by reason of being human, to make their own choices for their own reasons?

It is only slightly better to ask it this way: why do I think 28 or 29% of Hispanic voters voted for Trump on Election Night? This question I am prepared to answer.

During his campaign, Donald Trump made five fundamental promises:

- To put Americans and American jobs first, igniting an economic boom
- To stop illegal immigration ("Build the wall!") and enforce our laws
- To end foreign wars and large scale overseas U.S. involvement
- To fight the special interests in the D.C. swamp and make politicians accountable to the people who elected them
- And to re-fund the U.S. military and rebuild rotten American infrastructure

If accomplished, all of these actions would benefit Americans both native-born and legal immigrants, especially the hardworking labor and middle classes left behind during the first and second waves of globalization and since the great Financial Crisis of 2008. The Americans who work hard in construction, energy and other manual labor-intensive fields but lack pensions or retirement savings; the Americans surrounded by drug crime who want safer neighborhoods for their kids; the Americans who want better schools, including charter schools, but know that the unions (the Democratic party) stand in the way of progress; the hard working Americans who care more about the falling levels of their bank accounts than the rising levels of our oceans. To wit, the return of the American dream - an abstract concept central to the unique appeal of this nation to its own people and to all people.

The above passage describes many, many Hispanic Americans. These issues resonated with them throughout the 2016 Presidential Election campaign, especially the immigration issue.

To believe that better economic opportunities for all Americans regardless of educational background, safer neighborhoods and better schools are things that only White non-Hispanic Americans want would be one of the most racist political conclusions one could draw from Trump's victory in 2016. The continued failure of the Democratic Party to accept that that is true, make changes in its platform and offer real political solutions - real change - explains much of its national failures over the last ten to twenty years.

There was one bright moment for the DNC - 2008 to 2010 - when they had elected the Man and they had a mandate for change. And what did they give Americans? Higher health insurance premiums. Yes, the Obama Administration did help restore the foundations of American prosperity post 2008 but it was only the upper middle classes and the privileged few who really benefited. In this country, you cannot ask a thirty-eight year old construction worker to be satisfied with better benefits when there are not enough projects to go around due to regulations. You cannot ask a thirty-eight year old working (not disabled) single mother of three kids in elementary, middle and high school to trust you when she's worried about drugs and gangs. You cannot ask those things when you live in a cushy suburb and spend more time voicing support for those breaking the law. Or maybe you can, but just don't expect them to vote for you.

Moving onward. On Election Night, 27% of Asian Americans who voted chose Donald Trump. According to Edison Research's data, the figure was 29%. Why did so many voters in this category, who mostly come under the heading of "visible minority," and most of whose grandparents were not born in the United States, vote for an immigration-bashing demagogue on the right?

Once again, I am not certain. I am not Asian but I do have some opinions on the subject.

More than any other race or group in America, Asian Americans accept freedom without imposing their points of view and their decisions on others. Asian are not asking someone else to change; they are asking to be left alone without discrimination. They do not want or need your help, and they aren't asking for it. This is freedom and independence at the same time. They know their rights and they use them, like when an Asian American plaintiff sued Harvard University for improperly excluding superlatively qualified Asian students. Asian Americans have their values and they live them just like every other American group. But their stance, or should I say attitude, comes at little cost to other groups.

That is, unless you believe in zero sum analysis, in which case their very presence in the United States (let alone their disproportionate academic and financial successes) is a threat to more settled segments of the American nation.

Despite the fact that prior to the Immigration and Nationalisation Act of 1965 the Asian American (East Asian, South Asian or Pacific) population numbered around one million, by 2000 there were more than eleven million Asian Americans. In that year, according to labor market data compiled by the U.S. Census Bureau, 11% of Asian Americans were self employed. Only Whites had a higher percentage, 12.8%.

In 2008, 12.8% of MD physicians were Asian Americans. According to the Association of American Medical Colleges, by 2019 that figure had jumped to 17.1%. Business ownership continued to rise during that time frame, growing to almost two million. Somehow, Asian Americans achieved middle class status very quickly and they did so in a way that did not demand much from other American groups.

I call this the Freedom Project. Put simply, one becomes free by accepting freedom's powers and responsibilities. On its most basic level, that means looking after yourself, mate. Cue the Aussie accent. Food, clothing, shelter and work - all without violence. But these are merely man's most basic needs.

On a deeper level, freedom is a quest, an adventurous search for greener pastures, new rivers, greater opportunities. To wit, freedom is the quest for more freedom. As Albert Camus put it, "Freedom is nothing else but the chance to be better, whereas enslavement is the certainty of the worst."

This is what led pioneering societies to leave what they knew to embrace the unknown. Pioneering societies always begin with a group of families seeking freedom. The passionate desire to have a better future for your kids than present circumstances promise has led millions to walk over mountains, cross harsh deserts and roaring oceans, to face down and overcome wild beasts and hostile peoples in order to find something they had never seen before - something they could not have been capable of dreaming. And yet, there it was.

But on a deeper level still, freedom demands that we set others free. This constitutes the higher moral function of freedom - its sacred duty. Any man or woman who enjoys freedom must take care of himself or herself first; then he or she must take care of his or her family - parents, descendants, kith and kin. Freedom becomes truly transformative when it comes to the aid of those who live outside of our domestic walls - neighbors and strangers. We who love freedom are called to set them free. Setting them free most often takes common, tangible forms: providing them with good employment, working together to accomplish private goals, sharing life's joys and sorrows. All of this voluntary private action is freedom incarnate. The Freedom Project.

But there is a higher level still: "Greater love has no man than this, that a man lay down his life for his friends."

One may note that the Freedom Project includes economic activity. This is natural. Work is labor that creates products humans or animals need or want, or labor that provides necessary or desired services. Because work is necessary and good, all labor is noble. But not all ownership and management methods are noble. Only ownership and management methods that respect workers' dignity and rights are noble. The rest are base, exploitative ventures that rob men and women of their freedom in exchange for what these workers produce. Thus Camus pointed out, "If someone takes away your bread, he suppresses your freedom at the same time. But if some takes away your freedom, you may be sure that your bread is threatened, for it depends no longer on you and your struggle but on the whim of a master."

Accordingly free, contractual (= voluntary) economic activity is the necessary outworking of individual freedom, which produces free culture and a free civilization.

More than most other American groups, Asian Americans have taken readily to the Freedom Project. They have worked to provide for themselves and their families with little dependence on public resources. Further, they have worked to improve their levels of skills, knowledge, τέχνη to enable themselves to produce more and better goods, and provide more and more valuable (= powerful and/or effective) services. Justifiably they have prospered in a land of freedom.

So why might many of them have voted for Donald Trump? On one hand, Candidate Trump sold himself as a businessman with business skills he could use to fix America's very public problems. Rightly, in their views (perhaps) but certainty in mine, did Trump point out that the politicians who created these public problems could never be relied upon to fix them. Solutions could only come from an outsider, and there never was a bigger political outsider than he!

On the other hand, the very ethos of the Democratic Party is group-oriented. More specifically, it is non-elective-group-oriented: race, biological sex, national origin. Certain groups belong; certain groups receive favor. Ironically, this list of groups does not include the nuclear family, the most powerful non-elective group each person belongs to. Further, the Democratic Party, with the notable exception of its defense of homosexual rights, intentionally positions itself against choice-based identities and issues. Democrats call for greater governmental control over certain groups (gun owners, hedge funds, parents) and greater financial support for certain groups only (the poor, abortion clinics, state employees).

In contrast, the Freedom Project is individual-oriented. Any person can choose to embrace it. Choice is freedom.

Accordingly, the Democratic Party's pitch to voters in 2016 followed the same game plan outlined above: calls for greater governmental control and greater governmental financial support, made to certain groups only. Senator Hillary Rodham Clinton well-embodied this pitch. I suspect for many Asian Americans this was a non-starter.

The main group Donald Trump ostensibly marketed his campaign to were Americans. No hyphens. (No pun.) Trump was selling a product that *any* American could buy. Just like they could rent the penthouse suite in the Trump Plaza Hotel of yore, so long as they had the money.

In a way, this constitutes Trump's idea of national unity. We are all Americans with the same rights and privileges. No special classes (except businesses). No free rides. No exceptions. Because we are all exceptional, we all get treated the same. We are all Americans!

The Democratic Party's vision of national unity is notionally similar, but with an important, fatal, twist: we are all Americans with the same rights and privileges, they also claim. But they add that we are all part of different sex, racial, ethnic and other groups with different experiences within the greater American story. Each group's experience is valid. (I am with them up to here.) Then, fatally, they assert that because *certain* groups got ahead and others did not we must ignore the causes of injury or evil in *particular* cases and craft *general* remedies that go against the fundamental democratic principle of EQUAL JUSTICE UNDER LAW.

To wit, collective justice.

I do not support collective justice or its inverse, collective guilt. The Holy Bible, which I revere as God's revealed Word to humanity, communicating Who He Is and what we need to do in response to His revelation of Himself in the person of Jesus Christ, supports collective justice from a certain point of view. I will not get into examples here for the sake of clarity within the context of American politics. But also because the discussion does not alter my conclusion not to support this notion.

I do not support it because mankind is fundamentally flawed due to sin; he is not capable of doing justice as God does justice: impartial yet tempered with mercy. Nor can men or women redeem themselves from the penalty of breaking God's law. We need a Savior Who must come from outside of our paradigm to rescue us.

Because I know that humans are completely incapable of doing universal justice on our own, I prefer political systems that try to do justice in individual cases. On this smaller scale there is less room for error to reign. There is a greater chance that justice will be done.

This is whyI reject the whole panoply of Democratic Party-created privileges, from affirmative action to reparations to political correctness. While these are noble attempts to do collective justice, they each in turn inflict collective wrong on entire classes or groups of people who are not guilty as a class. I am not Hindu. I do not believe certain people are born into guilty classes that they cannot escape at all through any means during their lives. Obviously, there are guilty members of every class that man has designed but from the human perspective - the Western humanist perspective - they became guilty through their own actions. We cannot punish an entire class. We cannot punish an entire race. Would not we seem like Nazis if we did?

How doubly ironic, then, that Donald Trump would be called out as one of the most divisive U.S. Presidents ever when Trump's notion of American national unity is actually colorblind. (I believe both of these assertions are just.)

But the Democratic Party's actions will have more lasting consequences. The persistent refusal of the Democratic Party to resolve the existential political conflict of individual rights versus collective identities, costs them votes. It may also cost them the presidential election in 2020.

The phrase "Together we can" falls on deaf ears among the individually-minded. And the individually-minded - those of working age - are less likely to need government support. They are more likely to work in the private sector. They are more likely to choose alternatives rather than standard issue, one-size-fits-all solutions. More likely to be independent. But before we move on to discussing why Trump won more independents [sic] than Clinton on Election Night, I feel compelled to make one more point about Asian Americans.

Large numbers of Asian Americans are evangelicals. Bible-believing Christians. Faithful soldiers in the Christian Right. Individuals and families who care more about fighting abortion than immigration reform. Trump was their candidate.

The fact that the Democratic Party completely ignores, downplays or, frankly, holds in contempt the Christian faith as a part of the individual and collective identities of Americans who are not Whites causes them to lose the votes of these devoted persons. "Good riddance!" I can (and have) heard some Democrats say. "They're crazier than crazy. We don't need them anyway." Really? How many Asian Americans live in Wisconsin?

Further, it was a demonstration of political genius that Donald J. Trump could simultaneously be an anti-immigrant but pro-evangelical candidate. He did not come out the worse for wear over this painful moral compromise. We evangelicals did.

Independent Voters

According to exit polls, Trump won 46% of independents. That is 4% greater than for Clinton. How did Trump win independents?

Being independent politically is both an attitude and a disposition. The disposition is one that seeks to balance two extremes. It is one that is willing to compromise. It is a moderate disposition.

The attitude is a defiant stance against the Either/Or, black or white, football or baseball, binary social make up within the American soul. We Americans are hardwired to experience rivalry between two dominant social groups. This is the "Hatfields versus the McCoys" phenomenon. The Earps versus the Clantons. Applied to politics, it explains the refusal to choose between the two national effective (only they get people in statewide or national office throughout the country) political parties. This attitude is not juvenile. It is actually very American in its thought, but it harkens back to a different America: the nineteenth century nation expanding without limit towards the Pacific Ocean. Then, individuals and families confronted multiple geographic choices when it came to choosing their identities. Then, America was much more a patchwork of groups with differing values and ways of life than now. In this way, freedom coupled with diversity produced independent thinking. And independent thinking produced innovation.

No longer, unfortunately. The commercial homogenization of the American nation, the seeds of which were sowed by the New Deal, the bones and infrastructure of which were created during World War II to meet the challenge of global conflict and win, the forces of which were unleashed domestically in the post-war population and commercial boom revolutionized the thoughts and emotions that play out within the American soul. Now this nation of "rugged individualists" axiomatically accepts one-size-fits-all solutions to fundamental human problems, like the problem of how to finance the retirement of workers too old to continue intensive labor. And they accept government stewardship of those solutions. As a result, our nation became more uniform but less interesting. Difference makes for what is interesting.

Thankfully, we remain largely a free nation. We have access to data that points to and supports alternatives. We have means (though not as unrestricted as the Constitution calls for) of disseminating this data in real time to as large an audience as technology allows. (In 1776, the forerunner of the internet was a gazette - a cheap publication that quickly got information to subscribers or to purchasers on the street without the need of license or approval. This is what the freedom of the press enshrined in the First Amendment was designed to protect.) Thus the homogenization outlined above is not irreversible. Our future health and prosperity as a free nation depends on it.

Political independents, then, are the seeds of this counterrevolution, and their numbers have been growing steadily since 2004.

Why did more independents vote for Donald Trump than for Senator Hillary Clinton? Initially, let's look at the demographics of independent voters. I am certain the reader will be surprised a minimum of two times by the actual facts of who makes up independent voters. More than any other group, independents hide in our midst. There are no physically-observable characteristics which communicate to passers-by, "Hi. I am a political independent." You may even have come across some wearing those obnoxious red MAGA hats!

According to the Pew Research Center, American voters are more likely to be independents if they are male, White - Hispanic *and* non-Hispanic - agnostic, millennial, and suburban, with annual earnings between $40,000 and $99,000. First, biological sex. According to this research, men are almost 10% more likely to be independents than women. The next highest category for men is Republican. A scant 26% of men among more than 4,300 who were polled in November 2016 identified as Democrats.

Next, racial and ethnic identity. It may come as no surprise that the majority of White non-Hispanic Americans polled identified as Republicans. It may also come as no surprise that the majority of Hispanic Americans and Asian Americans identified as Democrats. However, 35% of White Americans polled identified as independents. And 32% of both Hispanics and Asians identified as independents. In other words, with African Americans excepted, fully one third of the U.S. electorate was independent in 2016. On Election Night, statistically one out of every three persons voting who was not Black was neither a Republican or a Democrat. That is a massive voting block, and it translates into massive political power. But it gets better.

Now onto African Americans. We provide (once again) the contrast to the above picture. But not by much. Twenty-six percent of African Americans polled in November 2016 identified as independents. This means that *more than one quarter of the entire American electorate is independent.*

Fittingly, though, this is not uniformly so. The next category I examined was religious belief. Not *beliefs.* Any type of organized faith in a Higher Power or Powers goes into the Faith category. The opposite - anti-Faith or atheism - goes into another category. The two other categories I examined were agnostic and "Nothing in particular," which I have labeled as the "Shoulder Shrugs", i.e., "It doesn't matter to me", "It's not relevant in my life", or "I don't really care".

Statistically, there are almost double the number of Shoulder Shrugs than agnostics or atheists combined. Forty-five percent of Shoulder Shrugs are independents regardless of age, biological sex or race. Among agnostics, fully 50% self-identify as independents. This is the second highest response rate to the question of being an independent among all categories assessed. Only one category out of perhaps seventy-five polls higher among independents than agnostics.

The one category that polls higher among independents than agnostic is "Total unaffiliated [religiously] millennials." Fifty-one percent of the youngest block of voters who do not practice a religion identify as independents. This is more than a demographic shift; this is a new paradigm.

This is really good news for all free thinkers, innovators, reformers, young people and those interested in them. More than one quarter of American voters are willing to buck the system and try something different. As one focuses on the younger generations of voters (ages 18-51 in 2016), the percentage increases to 38.5%! Cue Donald J. Trump.

So why did Donald Trump win more independents than Senator Clinton did? I believe there are three main reasons: first, by 2016 most Americans were fed up with "Business as usual" in Washington, D.C.. Politics had moved beyond disappointment into a place of disheartening corruption. Special interests reigned through their lobbyists and lawyers (not always the same persons), and common sense was nowhere to be found. While rank and file Democrats and Republicans to a large extent had made peace with that, independents had not. In fact, the very act of choosing to be an independent was a rejection of politics as usual.

Then along came Donald Trump, crass and extremely wealthy, unquestionably skilled at making money in one of the toughest markets on the planet - N.Y.C real estate. He was a known commodity, like his casinos. When one adds to his name a set of unorthodox policy positions for a twenty-first century Republican (e.g., protect Social Security, cut business and environmental regulations while increasing immigration restrictions, promise increased infrastructure spending and military spending) what developed was a very different political proposition. It was as if Trump was reversing the old 1950's adage attacked so well by Ronald Reagan, "Trust me. I'm from the government," into the statement, "We can't trust them. They're politicians. I'm not."

This is the type of marketing that appeals to independents. "I'm a businessman," Trump said many times in various ways. And what is a businessman to his fellow Americans? Level-headed, practical, trustworthy, accessible, hardworking, prosperous. In a word, exactly how most Americans view themselves regardless of race, sex, or religion. Donald Trump did an excellent job packaging himself in this role. He also did an excellent job using a sledgehammer to smash the sacred cows and other taboos surrounding us politicians: that we have specialized knowledge the public lacks; that we have experience necessary for legislating and governing that our neighbors do not have; that we are somehow worthy to rule over our fellows. In the near future, it will be very hard for us to reconstruct those necessary myths that support a ruling class in a free society.

Second, Trump's campaign targeted special interests. To most Americans, special interests appear like very real cartoon villains - not just bad but caracatursitically evil, larger than life, dressed in black or flaming red, with fire and brimstone. And while we speak of a range of "special interests," we can only identify two or three. This makes sense because a person cannot get angry at the abstract. It is the real, the concrete, the effective that offends and incenses. Planned Parenthood. The Oil & Gas lobby. The Environmentalists. Wall Street. These are probably America's top four most hated special interests.

But there is a degree of hypocrisy in this. Special interests only exist because someone has given money to support a public cause - that is to say a cause of interest to several members of the public. The money is used to educate, inform, convince and/or persuade those who control the tax purse strings and the regulatory red pens. Anyone who has ever supported a local nonprofit or community venture is implicated in this scheme. The goodness, justice or morality of the cause, politically, is not relevant. The popularity of the cause is the only relevant factor. That and the ability of government to further or to frustrate the cause.

Special interests are not the measure of government corruption or of our own corruption. They are the measure of our political effectiveness as a free, individual consumer-focused society. They exist to give what most of us really want from the government but are afraid to admit in daylight: increasing entitlements without increasing responsibilities; gas-guzzling environment-destroying identity badges; fat retirement accounts with zero accountability for how the money got there; the death of inconvenient truths.

And one more thing: to keep our neighbors whom we don't like from getting what they want. These are the reasons why millions of dollars flow voluntarily from American pockets to special interests. Daily. Even during recessions.

We are the special interests!

Third, Trump cast himself in the mold of a political outsider who was going to clean up the system. Since independents reject the political status quo, this strategy is more likely to appeal to them. Independents are less hypocritical than either Republicans or Democrats, because in a two party system, when you choose to be independent, you choose to lose. You choose to give up wide-scale support and financial leverage of working with the big guys. You choose to give up having a say during primary season in most U.S. states, including Florida. You choose to be labeled, "Other." But independents get to stand up for what they believe in without having to make the compromises necessary for the two party system to work. Independents who favor more open, more inclusive immigration policies but who hate abortion don't have to support both. Independents who believe in balanced budgets and smaller government spending, including less military spending, do not have to compromise. Instead, they just choose whichever candidate is likely to give them what they want. This is very practical, very business-like. It's the opposite of how politics works.

A political outsider openly attacking the status quo as corrupt is more likely to woo voters who have effectively rejected the two party system. The political insider is left on stage holding the bag. She (in this instance) had to persuade a block of voters who rejected affiliating with her party (as well as the other guys' party) that the status quo was fine and needed to continue.

Among young people this task was especially hard. Beginning in the 1950's, young persons in America began to reject the status quo *en masse* regardless of the category or institution. They grew up into the Baby Boomers we know and love (or loathe), and they produced a new and unique culture within the United States. In politics, the Baby Boomers gave us ever-expanding federal entitlements and abortion on demand throughout the nation. They gave us a global military footprint (even after the debacle of Vietnam) with a "defense" budget that is larger than most other countries' GDP's. They gave us commercial-driven TV culture and the twenty-four hour news cycle. In many senses, they turned us on and no one has figured out how to turn us back off again.

Some millennials reject this culture. Others embrace it. Some even carry the flag, and try to expand government entitlements to healthcare and lifestyle subsidization beyond the horizon. In the main, though, I believe millennials (saddled with student debt, living in cushy suburbs with mom and step-dad but too poor to afford a first home, and unfulfilled at work) were more likely to reject the status quo on November 8, 2016 than to vote to sustain it. It was crushing them, crushing their hopes and dreams. And this Clinton on the stage did not "feel your pain." She was more likely to have told them, just like their Boomer grandparents have done,

"Grow up!" Grow up and live in the world that I have broken for you using the democratic governance I have broken for you, with its runaway healthcare and education costs and poisoned rivers, but I won't take responsibility for it. Meanwhile, the Donald said, as it were, "The System is broken; it is rotten to the core. She built it. And she is rotten to the core. But I am going to fix it. It's going to be great. We're going to have brand new everything and no Mexicans, but Mexico will pay for it. We will make America great again."

Independents were listening.

What about education? Common sense (our own prejudices manipulated by a partisan media) tells us that Donald Trump won the votes of "undereducated" people and lost the votes of educated people. Once again, this collective assumption proved to be false.

The majority of American adults lack a college degree. (It also means that they lack huge college debts, but that is another subject!) Exit polling data from Edison Research (>23,000 participants) and from CNN (>24,000 participants) shows that 50% of Americans who voted on Election Night did not have a college degree. Eighteen percent of Americans who voted had a post-college graduate degree (Masters, JD, PhD, MD, DO, DPharm, etc.). While according to CNN Donald Trump did win a greater share of votes of persons who lack a college degree, that share was only 51%. That's slightly more than half. Meanwhile, according to Edison Research, Hillary Clinton won 46% of votes from Americans who did not pursue education past high school at all. This is hardly what we have been led to assume. In fact, the only education category which approached a landslide victory was post-college graduate degree. According to both polls, Clinton won 58% of those Americans' votes. But Trump won 37%. This is greater than a third. So even here, we do not see the stark polarization of political support by education painted by the media.

The Money Factor

Finally, there is one last factor to be analyzed in order to determine how Donald Trump won the presidency in 2016: money. Once again, the numbers yielded surprising insights.

I believe the average reader of this book, like I did, assumed that Donald Trump won a greater percentage of votes from wealthier people than Hillary Clinton did on November 8, 2016. But that is false.

I believe the average reader of this book, like I did, assumed that the suburban vote was the true geographic battleground, with the winner barely edging out his rival. But that is also false.

Finally, I believe the average reader of this book, like I did, assumed the money race between the two main presidential candidates would be close. False.

The truth is that Donald Trump won the middle class vote, the only vote that actually means something in our election system. The middle class has numbers, education, means and advocacy. From their ranks arise both the soldiers and the generals behind every community, statewide or national volunteer campaign (a military word) and public policy crusade. Moreover, the middle class has at least one type of "property" - be it a house or an apartment they own, or a professional degree that provides for direct entry into high-paying skilled work, or a 401(k) and other savings. This means they do not depend on the government for benefits. It also means they can withstand adverse government policies on certain issues unlike the dependent classes.

As long as we remain a free country, whichever presidential candidate persuades more of these propertied working people to support him or her will win every election. Period.

On November 8, 2016, Donald Trump did so. According to CNN exit polling data, a greater share of persons who earned $50,000 or more voted for Trump than Clinton. But according to the same polling data, Clinton won a greater share of persons who earned $200,000 or more per year.

Not all polls showed that Senator Clinton won more votes from the nation's top earners. Three other polls showed that Clinton and Trump tied for support among the country's wealthiest families. But CNN's data was based on surveys of more than 24,000 people. Thus I find it more persuasive.

Median household income in 2015 was $54,000. In addition, based on 2016 U.S. census data, households that earned between $50,000 and $100,000 - a category that all polls show Trump won - constitutes between the 46.75th percentile and the 75th percentile in terms of earnings, i.e., the middle of the scale. Therefore, because Donald Trump won this block he won the middle class.

Given this, one may not be surprised to learn that Donald Trump won 5% more suburban votes than Hillary Clinton. So said polling data from Edison Research.

"But what about the big money?" you may ask. What big money? Senator Hillary Clinton raised more than $500 million in campaign donations - *almost a quarter billion dollars* more *than billionaire Donald Trump raised.* So I ask again, What big money?

We conservatives often hear the argument that in the United States (like in New Zealand) we need to get the money out of politics. Elections would be funded by tax dollars (presumably after a candidate acquires a threshold number of signatures, else there would be no way (other than money) of gauging the seriousness of a person's campaign). We are told that if we did that elections would be more fair for the candidates. But I ask them, What could be more fair than a candidate outraising her opponent by *a quarter billion dollars* and losing?

Are these liberals after fairness or do they really want control? Control of other people's money, which is to say their choice of which candidates to back? Under the current Supreme Court iteration of the law of the land, choice in politics is Constitutionally-protected speech; and to limit a person's speech (money) in this arena violates his, her or its constitutional rights.

Sure. While I might not agree that limits on our campaign donations should be imposed by fiat from someone who purports to sit over our heads, I do have a problem with our courts' inability to see the difference between money and the opinions that it supports.

Please note: the threshold for the top 1% of Americans in terms of income (excluding capital gains) for 2015 was $408,000. The threshold for the top 10% was approximately $200,000. Accordingly to exit polling data from CNN (>24,000 participants), Senator Clinton won a greater share of the top 10% than billionaire Donald Trump. To the extent that there was big money involved -

measured by total donations or by individual income - Clinton won that race. And lost the election.

Immigration

One last concluding set of thoughts: ominously, according to Roper Center polling data, for 64% of Americans who voted for Donald Trump on November 8, 2016, the single most important issue was immigration. According to CNN polling data, while only 25% of participants said illegal immigrants should be deported, more than 80% of those voters voted for Donald Trump. The next most important issue, according to Roper's poll, was terrorism. Further, according to CNN's polling data, 42% of Americans who voted on Election Night thought international trade took away American jobs; almost two-thirds of these voters voted for Donald Trump. In other words, for many American voters and for the majority of Trump's voters our way of life is threatened by a nameless, faceless, brown external Other. This does not bode well for our country.

These are the complex, paradoxical demographics of Donald Trump's victory. Without irony, they reveal the simplicity of his message.

In politics, the simplest messages are the most powerful. And the more abstract the subject, the greater the resonance:

"The only thing we have to fear is fear itself."
"Ask not what your country can do for you, but ask what you can do for your country."
"I have a dream today."

These are among the most powerful political messages in human history. They are simple and abstract.

"Mr. Gorbachev, tear down that wall!" This message is simple, but concrete rather than abstract. It did not outlive its context, although it did prove to be both iconic and successful.

"Build the wall! Build the wall! Build the wall!" Ominous and aggressive, as mentioned above, and certainly ironic for a nation that calls itself "The Arsenal of Freedom" to build a wall to defend itself. And yet there it is.

But the most powerful slogan of the 2016 Presidential Election cycle was not, "Build the wall!" Nor was it, "I'm with her." It was, "Make America Great Again." A statement, not a campy shout, that went to the heart of the problem as seen by millions of Hispanic, Asian, Black and White voters. It was a statement that launched a thrice married real estate billionaire and media mogul into the most powerful position on Planet Earth; a statement written in simple white letters against a red background on cheap baseball caps manufactured in China and sold to Trump supporters most likely for a profit. All of which point clearly to the issues that lay directly ahead during Trump's administration.

LESSONS: liberalism is concentrated; conservatism is diffused. This helps conservatives win the electoral college; this dupes liberals into thinking if they can just win key parts of key states through demographic advantage rather than effective leadership, they can get into power and change the *culture* by legislation, because that is what they are after.

The chief weapon against this strategy is not voter registration "reform." Rather it is immigration restriction. Because native-born liberals have less children on average than conservatives and because the key drivers of larger families among liberals - Catholicism and Orthodox Judaism - are on the wane culturally, the inability of liberals to import people whom they can likely convince to join their political party leaves them dead in the water. At least in a democracy it does.

PART IV

••••••••••●•••••••••

THE TRUMP ADMINISTRATION, I

The Disruptor-in-Chief Takes Office

•••••••••●•••••••••

"If freedom had always had to rely on governments to encourage her growth, she would probably be still in her infancy or else definitively buried with the inscription 'another angel in heaven.' [W]hoever blindly entrusts [governments] with the care of freedom has no right to be surprised when she is immediately dishonored."
— Albert Camus, Bread and Freedom

On January 20, 2017, after noon, Donald John Trump (Senior) stood before United States Supreme Court Chief Justice John G. Roberts, placed his hand on the family Bible, and swore to uphold the U.S. Constitution and faithfully execute the Office of the Presidency of the United States of America. Roberts's and Trump's words were broadcast live throughout the entire world, and their voices resonated through the streets of Washington, D.C.

By operation of law, Donald Trump was already president by the time he was sworn in. That took place automatically at twelve noon. The effect is to ensure a seamless transition of power from one man or woman to another. While the United States may not be unique in employing the law in this way, we were certainly the first nation in achieving what it is designed to protect: the peaceful transition of executive power and authority from one unrelated man to another. We were the first country in history to achieve this when, in 1797, the great George Washington left office and was replaced on

Saturday, March 4, 1797, by that short, scrappy, eloquent Yankee John Adams. It had never been done before peacefully, and it sent shockwaves through the gilt halls of Europe.

We have no record of how it was received throughout Africa or in China, Japan and other parts of Asia, the Pacific, Australia, and New Zealand. We do have on record the response of America's former king, George III, when confronted with the prospect of General George Washington resigning his commission at the close of the Revolutionary War. That George said of this one, "If he does that, he will be the greatest man on the earth."

Although Donald Trump's ascendancy to the presidency was neither epic nor as monumental as that of former President Barack Hussein Obama, it was a watershed moment in U.S. political history in many of its own respects. Donald Trump was the first non-politician - and thereby nonparty elitist - to be elected president since September 11, 2001, a date which marked the true beginning of America's twenty-first century. Trump was the first non-politician elected president since General Dwight D. Eisenhower (a career soldier) in 1952. Neither man had ever held political office at all before they were sworn in to the highest political office in the land.

Furthermore, unlike General Eisenhower, Donald Trump ran in the face of opposition from his party's elite and prevailed. This had never been done before in U.S. history. Even former California Governor Ronald Reagan had more backing from Republican leaders in 1980 when he ran to challenge President Jimmy Carter than Trump did during 2015 and 2016.

Thus for the first time this century and the first time since the television age began (1960), the U.S. president was a non-politician who operated in a manner openly hostile to both his party's ruling insiders and openly hostile to the opposition party's leaders. As will be seen below, this particular behavior almost turned into Trump's Achilles heel.

Rather than just a beginning, January 20, 2017, turned out to be the apogee of Donald Trump's first administration. From that day onward many of the dark, subterranean forces always brewing beneath the streets of Washington, New York, Chicago, San Francisco, and Los Angeles, burst forth and attempted to drown President Donald Trump. Other forces, though, President Trump unleashed on himself through his fault alone. Still other forces he unleashed on the American nation. We will examine all of these forces and draw our own conclusions.

Washington's Farewell Address

•••••••••●•••••••••

But let us begin with President Donald Trump's inaugural address. The inaugural address is easily a president's most important piece of rhetoric during his or her administration. The entire country pauses to recognize the transfer of federal executive power and authority. Presidents typically seize this moment to share some inspiring words or to offer their battle plan for the next four years.

The inaugural address is so important it is one of the few speeches presidents are typically remembered by. American journalists and historians have archived the inaugural addresses of all forty-five U.S. presidents. For most presidents, that is the only rhetoric they are known for. The exceptions are all noteworthy, beginning with George Washington, our very first president.

The preeminent man of his generation, George Washington, Esq., climbed upward from the ranks of Virginia's planter elite to become the first man in the nation. He amassed a sizeable fortune on his way to power. But he achieved political power by his willingness to serve, his majestic presence, his indomitable temper, and his refusal to yield to anyone on earth. It did not matter the odds or the consequences. That being said, Mr. Washington was no wild boar from the backwoods. A learned and cultured man, he could write communiques and letters to foreign powers in fluent French and at his first inaugural ball, he took the time to dance with every lady who was present.

Ironically, perhaps, the words for which George Washington is most remembered were from his last public address. Fittingly they were never spoken by their author. Rather, President Washington chose to have them published in a newspaper, which came out on September 19, 1796.

In its day and for more than a century afterward it was more widely reprinted than the Declaration of Independence. It stood as a monument to Washington's greatness and to his surprisingly, refreshingly moderate policy views. Now, however, it is worse than forgotten. It is unknown.

It is fitting now that we re-examine President Washington's principles of public policy as set forth in his Farewell Address, because they will both illuminate how Washingtonian some of President Trump's policies are. But they will also help reveal the several incongruities between the moderation our country's founder counseled in the name of liberty and independence, justice and humanity, virtue, peace, and lasting American prosperity and the actions his 44th successor in office took in the name of these same values.

According to his Farewell Address, President Washington elicited the principles below during forty-five years of near continuous service to the nation he helped found. His service as surveyor, militia colonel, land speculator, planter, merchant, manufacturer, burgess, delegate and President of the Continental Congress, commanding general of the United States Army, President of the Constitutional Convention, and first President of the United States of America exposed this Virginian to all aspects of American life and took him to every part of the new nation. He believed these principles, as well as the actions he took in their name, would stand up manfully under scrutiny, even by posterity. Indeed, President Washington expressly evoked countless future generations, hoping

105

that the nation he founded would "never cease" to regard with kindness the sentiments expressed in this address.

Washington's first principle was national union through one government. According to our founding father, having a single national government was what made Americans Americans and not merely residents of a particular state. For Washington, "slight shades of difference" in "religion, manners, habits, and political principles" did not alter the essential fact that Americans constitute a single nation. The crucible of war, with its dangers to life and property and its necessary bloodshed and sacrifice, were born jointly by Americans from all quarters. It was the mysterious instrument that God used to forge the whole. Now that the war was won, common interest counseled that Americans "preserve the union of the whole." For Washington, this unity was the main pillar for our independence - politically, economically and socially.

A necessary corollary of this unity was equal protection of the national laws regardless of a person's state of residence or where he or she does business. In Washington's own language he called this "equal laws of a common government." Neither a citizen in his business nor a state in its interest would suffer the indignity of unequal treatment from partisan or sectarian opposition.

Another important corollary - perhaps the most surprising for a native-born son of Old Virginia who never visited Europe and whose forebears back to four generations had lived in America - was that immigration and naturalization helped make new Americans equal in rights, affections, and duties to their native-born neighbors. In very few words, President Washington established this notion as part of his principle of unity:

> Citizens, by birth or *choice,* of a *common* country,
> that country has a right to concentrate your
> *affections.* The name of American, which belongs to
> you in your *national* capacity, must always exalt the
> just pride of patriotism more than any appellation
> derived from local discriminations.

Citizenship, then, and affections were paramount for George Washington and not national origin or region of residence. Moreover, pride in being American, a name that for Washington only applied justly on a national level, should outweigh all local distinctions.

With this robust unity of government, then, Americans might frame their economic and social intercourse in order to build a strong, independent, prosperous nation, with each region of the country building upon its strengths whether commercial, manufacturing or agricultural and employing honest trade under equal laws with the other regions to create balance, harmony, mutual interest and wide-spread prosperity.

Because of its potential to help Americans build a prosperous but independent future, President Washington foresaw that this principle of national union under one government would be most attacked by the enemies of the new nation, whether foreign or domestic. And he counseled spiritual, psychological and emotional weapons with which to combat those efforts to weaken this union.

For two generations, Americans regardless of political party or region heeded President Washington's counsel and forged an ever-expanding union of American citizens stretching across the continent. Other statesmen such as U.S. Senators Daniel Webster and Sam Houston, and President Andrew Jackson stood up for the principle of national union at all costs: "I feel in the depths of my soul that it is the highest, most sacred, and most irreversible part of my obligation to preserve the **union** of these states, although it may cost me my life." Senator Webster put it most simply and elegantly, and thus most powerfully: "liberty and union, now and forever, one and inseparable."

That phrase captures the echo of President Washington's idea of unity.

And then a third generation arose that knew not Washington or revolution or foreign invasion. A generation that regarded sectional interests and distinctions more and more critically and with less tolerance. A generation that lacked the hard schooling in war and diplomacy that counseled patience and forbearance. A generation that replaced speeches with cannons.

The next three principles served as the pillars of President Washington's foreign policy and the foreign policy of the United States until the twentieth century - a century of forgetfulness. These principles are to avoid entering into other nations' disputes with other nations; to promote just and peaceful relations with all nations; and to forge no permanent alliances.

From Washington's perspective, these principles not only supported national independence, but they fulfilled "the obligation which justice and humanity impose on every nation." Namely, good faith, justice and peace with all nations.

Washington found it unreasonable to suppose that a nation would not act in its own best interest. What he demanded of his nation and of other nations in their relations was justice. But what he counseled his young nation was restraint. Washington and his fellow founders were very familiar with the decline and fall of ancient republics and mediaeval kingdoms and the supposed causes of these political catastrophes. They were also familiar with the weaknesses of human nature and how these could cause national downfall. One major way to avoid such a fate was to enter into as few alliances as possible and no permanent ones. Also to maintain such just relations with neighbors so as to give no offense that could serve as a pretext for war.

For more than a hundred years, with few exceptions, the United States strove to uphold these principles of foreign policy. Departure from these policies during the twentieth century introduced the permanent income tax, large permanent defense expenditures, permanent debt, permanent inflation and other evils Washington foresaw and counseled against.

One famous voice in the halls of power in our nation's capital during the mid-twentieth century specifically asked what President Washington would have thought of contemporary defense arrangements. I think he would have been appalled. *A fortiori* today.

The next principle would come as a shock to most Reagan-era Republicans and to almost all post-September 11 Republicans: avoid "overgrown [sic] military establishments." For Washington, an armed force that outgrew its reasonable size became a threat to liberty under a republican government. Instead, Washington offered the power of national union as a stronger bulwark than multiplying men at arms.

Critics of our own era might chuckle at this seemingly antiquated or perhaps even anachronistic political principle. Our era began with a world war that ended as a practical matter the ability of the United States to isolate itself from the greater world and its entanglements. But before they consign it to the dustbin of history, they should recall a few critical facts. First, the President who endorsed this principle was our nation's first military commander-in-chief. As indicated earlier, he chose to step down at the end of the American war for independence at a moment when he was the most powerful man on an entire continent. He did so rather than either seizing ultimate political power by violence or accepting the grant of monarchical power held out to him by some of the crowd. If Washington had acted otherwise, he would have suffocated America's independence and civil rights while still in the crib. Moreover, President Washington had spent many years under arms. He was thoroughly familiar with the character of men who dispense violence and death upon another's orders. Even if we ourselves (most of whom are neither active duty military members or veterans) do not perceive such a danger, President Washington deserves the benefit of the doubt.

Second, at the time Washington penned these words no American city possessed a professional police force. Crime was prevented and criminal laws were largely enforced by voluntary self-help by the citizens. If a more serious threat arose, the state militia could be called out. Washington's words, though, should not be construed as an admonish against professional policing. But they absolutely should be interpreted as a warning against militarized police forces, which a great number of American cities have today.

When a body of men dressed in battle fatigues and armed to the teeth with military weapons and vehicles takes to the streets, liberty has already fled the scene. What important state interest could possibility be upheld through the use of this corps of armed men? Does anyone hold them accountable or are they a law unto themselves? Better to build the wall and seal off entry into our country than tolerate well-armed "soldiers" swaggering down the streets as if we were in some banana republic.

The next principle is to assure that each citizen does his or her duty and respects our laws. Duty was central to George Washington's concept of public service. Along with honour, it motivated him on multiple occasions to set aside the comforts of hearth and home and hazard his life and fortune in the name of liberty. Washington expected his fellow citizens to maintain similarly high standards of duty or at least to honour those who did. He also expected his fellow citizens without exception to submit to lawful authority and comply with the law's demands. For him, this was what true liberty meant. In this regard, Washington believed that the function of a free government was "to confine each member of the society within the limits prescribed by the laws, and to maintain all in the secure and tranquil enjoyment of the rights of person and property." Hardly the sentiments of a government-resenting libertarian.

Moreover, these duties to obey lawful authority and respect the laws of the land were sacred to Washington's heart. As such the duty to obey the law, in Washington's worldview, was imbued with religious authority.

Embedded in his Farewell Address was the political principle that impelled George Washington and his fellow founders to fight the forces of the British crown. "The basis of our political systems [sic] is the right of the people to make and to alter their constitutions of government." This was the founding principle of an independent, free nation.

Next we move on to the principle for which Washington's Farewell Address is most remembered, save one. This principle was to resist the spirit of party or faction, which he called, "[a] fire not to be quenched." Washington spent several paragraphs laying out his analysis of the power of faction in democratic, republican and monarchical politics. In tracing the dangerous psychological effect of the spirit of party on popular opinion, democratic governance and freedom, President Washington must have had in mind the frequently consulted histories of the Greek city states and the Roman Republic. After all, Washington's compatriots and friends knew that he idolized the legendary Roman statesman Lucius Quinctius Cincinnatus, patrician, farmer and general, who left his plow in the field to answer the call of his fellow citizens to lead them in the defense of their fatherland. After achieving a brilliant victory, Cincinnatus returned to his farm, abandoning absolute control of the Roman state.

From Washington's point of view, the spirit of party was a part of human nature which, if not controlled, would lead to either the usurpation of political power from the people and/or the destruction of liberty itself. Parties of whatever origin or structure had the same aim: to frustrate, counteract, and ultimately control the deliberative and the elective functions of government. Factions substitute the will of the party for the will of the people. Factions turn honourable public administration into a mirror of the rising and falling fortunes of various groups. Factions led to dissension, dissension led to revenge, revenge led to crime, crime led to despotism and the loss of liberty.

One part of Washington's analysis of the dangers of faction rings so true today, that it deserves to be quoted in full. Further, I have placed it here in a chapter about the beginning of the administration of Donald Trump, because Washington's sage counsel serves almost as a prophecy of what would follow.

[The party spirit] serves always to distract the public councils and enfeeble the public administration. <u>It agitates the community with ill-founded jealousies and false alarms, kindles the animosity of one part against another, foments occasionally riot and insurrection.</u> *It opens the door to foreign influence and corruption, which finds a facilitated access to the government itself through the channels of party passions.* Thus the policy and will of one country are subjected to the policy and will of another.

Two hundred twenty years in advance, President Washington described Donald Trump's use of and impact on Twitter (see underlined) and described the dangerous influence which covert foreign intervention would have on Trump's administration and authority (see italics). But here I have gotten ahead of myself.

President Washington did acknowledge that political factions could indeed serve the cause of liberty. But he believed that beneficent effect to be reserved solely for monarchical political systems. Washington may have had in mind the previous great revolution in the English-speaking world, the Glorious Revolution of 1688, in which the Whig political faction persuaded a protestant foreign king to invade their own country so as to save them from the catholic despotism of King James II. But when it came to popular, elective governments, Washington thought the dangers of excess to be too great to risk cultivating the shady spirit.

Time and concision prevent me from addressing individually each of the principles Washington elicited (preserve separation of powers; promote habits of religion [sic] and morality; promote education; pay taxes and debts). Before we turn back to the inaugural address of Donald J. Trump, I am compelled to highlight one last principle, because it so chillingly overshadows the current administration.

This principle was to maximize foreign trade *without regard to politics.* Washington envisioned free trade with any who would trade peacefully with American merchants. Repeatedly in his Farewell Address he counseled against foreign alliances and favored trading *statii.* The way Washington saw it, "a passionate attachment of one nation for another produces a variety of evils." Europe specifically, since it was the focus of western international relations, was beset with conflicting interests and complicated alliances. From Washington's perspective on the Potomac, the United States should have nothing to do with that continent politically, while at the same time maximizing trade with all on equal terms.

If we attempt to place ourselves in Washington's shoes, this makes sense. Our first president spent most of his adult life struggling with the British against the French and their Native American allies, or struggling with the French against the British and many of those same First Nations. Further, George Washington had never visited Europe, unlike Ben Franklin, who spent nine years in France and one and a half decades in London; Franklin's son William would remain loyal to the British Crown and settle in England permanently after the Revolutionary War. Despite objectively yielding to the charms of cultivated individual Europeans like le Marquis de la Fayette and Mrs. Henrietta Liston, when it came to Europe or its nations as a whole, they were as alien to George Washington as the moon.

Not every founder was of this view. Thomas Jefferson, that great architect of the Declaration of Independence, of the Constitution of the Commonwealth of Virginia and of the University of Virginia, was passionately devoted to France, where he lived for almost five years. He followed closely the French Revolution from his vantage point along the Atlantic seaboard, cheering it on. In fact, three of the first five U.S. presidents all resided in France during the 1780's. From their points of view, certain European nations did share common interest with the young United States, while others did not. Would it not be a shame to let slip close ties when these could be used to build stronger, more favorable trading arrangements?

For Washington, the real danger was the use of favorable trade ties as a wide avenue for foreign influence to enter the United States and undermine her young institutions. Favored nation status and favorable trade deals led readily on the one hand to over generous concessions and the forgetting of one's own nation's interests, and on the other hand to ill-will among and potential retaliation from the excluded nations. Thus foreign influence would be brought to bear on the one side as well as the other. And the effects would be to alter the decisions of U.S. political institutions through the misleading of public opinion about where America's true interests lay. Moreover, Washington foresaw that ambitious and corrupt Americans would aid foreign nations in their efforts to influence the American people's elected representatives.

So clear was Washington's vision on the issue of foreign influence that the most trenchant passage on that subject in the Farewell Address will be quoted at length. Then it will be used to frame part of our discussion of the Trump Administration.

> Against the insidious wiles of foreign influence (I conjure you to believe me, fellow-citizens [sic]) the jealousy of a free people ought to be constantly awake, since history and experience prove that foreign infusion is one of the most baneful foes of republican government. But that jealousy to

be useful must be impartial; else it becomes the instrument of the very influence to be avoided, instead of a defense against it. Excessive partiality for one foreign nation and excessive dislike of another cause those whom they actuate to see danger only on one side, and serve to veil and seven second the arts of influence on the other. Real patriots who may resist the intrigues of the favorite are liable to become suspected and odious, while its tools and dupes usurp the applause and confidence of the people, to surrender their interests.

President George Washington would have had us avoid military interventions and political alliances abroad, while maximizing trade with as many nations as possible. He would have had us cultivate our minds through education, humble our souls through the Christian religion, and strengthen our character through duty and adversity. Above all, Washington, after whom the national capital city is named, would have ceaselessly striven to encourage us to remain politically and culturally united as one nation spanning a continent.

What of Donald Trump?

Trump's First Inaugural Address:

·········●●●●●●●●···

My first impressions were second hand; I did not watch the first Trump inauguration. I heard about it at church that weekend from two different friends who share my politics though not my generation (female in her 50's, male in his 60's) or my race. Both are White. I recall smiling pleasantly while listening to their reactions.

When I read the inauguration speech transcript for the first time, I confess I was surprised. It was more uniting and upbeat than I had expected. Trump was lofty in tone. He established clear targets for his first administration. He sought to embrace a wide audience. He addressed our nation, our allies and our enemies. He brought full circle the dominant campaign message he had been communicating since his very first speech on July 16, 2015: make America great again.

The themes of President Donald Trump's first inaugural address were unity, inclusion, and empowerment: the unity of our nation despite the arbitrary distinctions of race or ethnicity, and choice-based differences of opinion and lifestyle; the inclusion of all Americans into the national family and the national scheme of rights and rewards; the empowerment of all Americans to pursue their dreams without Washington standing in the way.

Themes

Unity: it is on the face of our money, which during bad times is what we Americans value most. E pluribus unum - "out of many, one." Nothing better expresses the founding idea Almighty God had when He birthed the American nation in 1776. This founding norm has been hard-pressed and betrayed; captured and enslaved; crucified; slaughtered. And yet she rises again!

Evermore, the American nation is one people made out of many peoples. This is also one of our sources of greatest strength.

Moreover, unity is Washingtonian. As we discussed earlier, our nation's first president identified national political union as the main pillar in America's house supporting our independence. In Washington's view, national political union provided security, peace, lasting prosperity and hope for the future. Further, in Washington's view this national political union represented and flowed out of social bonds transcending religion, geography and national origin. As mentioned earlier, for Washington differences in "religion, manners, habits, and political principles" were but "slight shades" that did not alter the essential fact that Americans make up a single nation.

President Donald Trump's first inaugural address reflected perfectly this notion of George Washington. President Trump voiced a concept of unity that embraced all Americans while acknowledging distinctives. President Trump sought to deploy unity in a great national effort to rebuild our country and restore its promise. While President Washington, no doubt, would have been more cautious in his estimation of our nation's great potential, some part of him would have assessented to this sentiment about unity that President

Trump voiced in his inaugural, "When America is united, America is totally unstoppable."

Inclusion: according to President Trump, the raison d'etre of free government is to serve its citizens - all of its citizens. In a nation that has always acknowledged possession of "unalienable" rights, including the pursuit of happiness, the question is not, "What do Americans need?" Rather the question should be, "What do Americans *want*?" And in this context, we mean what Americans want from the *government.*

President Donald Trump knew the answers. It is one of the chief reasons why he won the presidential election in 2016. And he did not fail to include them in his first inaugural address: <u>great schools, safe neighborhoods and good jobs</u>. That's it.

That is all most Americans want from the government. Figure out how to give voice these three notions and you will never lose an election. Figure out how to deliver these notions to the American people and there would be no stopping your political aspirations.

I call them notions, not rights, because I am conservative. I do not believe individuals possess the right to great schools. Yet I and most other Americans want great schools for our kids. I do believe we possess the right to have our government - the chief provider of schools in our country - put forth its best efforts for education with its best people. *That* is a right! I also believe in a right of equal access to great schools once a school has proven itself to be great. That means charter schools. That means allowing testing-based entrance to higher performing schools. That means vouchers to pay for access to better schools. *These* are rights.

Nor do I believe that we possess a right to live in a safe neighborhood. After all, what is safe? Who defines it? Does safe mean no crime or that only certain crimes do not occur? We have not decided. I still know this is what I want for my family and it is something I am familiar with.

I grew up in safe neighborhoods. The suburban upper middle class neighborhoods in western N.Y. where I was raised had little property crimes (theft, robbery, vandalism). I have no recollection of any crimes of violence (apart from kids fighting). But our neighborhoods had illegal drug use by White people, including by school-aged children. None of our White neighbors were prosecuted for drug crimes or any other crime. However, I remember hearing at school of kids being prosecuted for drug crimes. They were all Black and they did not live in any of my neighborhoods growing up. By the way, no kid in the neighborhood I grew up in had ever heard of Child Protective Services. So what gives?

We can all agree we do not want property crimes or violent crimes taking place in our neighborhoods at all. We can all agree it is our right to have the government (police) put forth its best efforts to do away with both of those types of crimes. But how far we wish the government (police) to go to eradicate *crime* is a question of enormous political and moral import. We do not all share the same desires in this area. We do not all have the same picture of what this would look like in practice. But we can all agree that we want our families to live in safe neighborhoods.

I certainly do not believe in any right to a good job - especially from the government. In our country, most jobs are private sector jobs which are governed mostly by private contract law. The way the system works, only qualified people get hired to work jobs. The more skills they have and the better they perform, the better the job they can expect to attain. That is the equation. It takes hard work, time, preparation, and experience, initiative. and risk. It is also subject to external forces like economic cycles, radical shifts in consumer demand, technological obsolescence, war, and natural disasters. Moreover, not all industries and sectors use the same pay scale.

It is surprising how often this equation does not work. How often quality skilled workers are passed over, marginalized or abandoned. How often the good opportunities go to friends and family rather than to loyal employees. How often human capital receives inhumane treatment. How often an honest day's work does not yield an honest day's pay. This plays a bigger role in our system than the simpleminded will admit.

The question remains, though: what to do about it? For mandates to have teeth, there must be accountability and sanction. Those are expensive for the state (taxpayers) in terms of resources and time and are burdensome to businesses. They slow down the hiring, review, and promotion processes. They sap spontaneity. They divert resources to "compliance" that could be spent on research and development.

For some, this is the price we must pay to ensure workers are not discriminated against in hiring and not treated poorly while on the job. But what is the opportunity cost? A decrease in freedom, a decrease in independence. For some, this will be worth the cost. For others, not so much. And for others, not at all.

I do not know most of the readers of this book. I do not know where their opinions lay in terms of those three categories I just identified. I do know that their opinions must go into one of those three categories. I also know with certainty they care about finding and keeping good jobs.

This brings us full circle. President Trump knew that the life aspirations of most Americans regardless of sex, race, ethnicity, social status, economic class, or any other marker boiled down to three things: great schools for our kids; safe neighborhoods to live in; and good paying and benefitting jobs. Then, as with his campaign rhetoric, he expanded his words to intentionally include individuals in very different circumstances.

> But for too many of our citizens, a different reality exists: mothers and children trapped in poverty in our inner cities; rusted out factories scattered like tombstones across the landscape of our nation; an education system flush with cash, but which leaves our young and beautiful students deprived of all knowledge; and the crime and the gangs and the drugs that have stolen too many lives and robbed our country of so much unrealized potential. This American carnage stops right here and stops right now.

Have other U.S. presidents evoked similar sentiments, seeking through speech to bring together individuals and families from walks of life so different they might only share nationality and oxygen? Without a doubt. But they were not Republicans and they would not have followed those words with these:

> We are one nation and their pain is our pain. Their dreams are our dreams. And their success will be our success. We share one heart, one home, and

one glorious destiny. The oath of office I take today
is an oath of allegiance to all Americans.

This type of We-are-all-one, social media-driven emotional reductionism is a product of the twenty-first century. It is novel. And it evolves continually. It was birthed through the tragedy of September 11, 2001, when our nation sought to draw together to stand against terror. In communities throughout our country and throughout the world, there were physical gatherings of strangers seeking to connect, to mourn, to heal, and to unite. I can still recall those precious moments, the depth of the pain but also the depth of the love for America and for my fellow Americans almost twenty years later.

And yet I also recall a woman asking during the aftermath how long this unity would last. It was not a rhetorical question. I am not sure what was going through her mind and heart at the time. She may have had a deep understanding of the complexities and paradoxes of American nationhood.

Or maybe it was gut instinct telling her that this one nation of individuals taken from so many others, with so many regions, so many different ways of being free, so diverse, like a teenager cannot sustain the emotion of unity for too long. She was right. As we have seen and as we will discuss the path ahead would be littered with many casualties of our nation's unwillingness to weld freedom and liberty with justice and equality.

The two strongest verbs in Trump's first inaugural address were *rebuild* and *restore*. In the second paragraph of his address - which was the first paragraph after preferatory, thankful remarks, President Donald Trump said, "We, the citizens of America, are now joined in a great national effort to rebuild our country and restore and restore its promise to all our people."

If President Donald Trump directed his inaugural address to a specific group rather than all Americans, our allies and our enemies, it was the marginalized and forgotten. From the outset of his speech, President Trump spoke directly to them with words of encouragement: "the forgotten men and women of our country will never be forgotten again." "This is your celebration," said President Trump, referring to all Americans. "You will never be ignored again."

President Donald Trump only used the personal pronoun "I" three times in his entire address. He first used it to refer to the oath of office he had just taken. He immediately turned the focus of the phrase inside out: "The oath of office I take today is an oath of allegiance to all Americans." Once again, President Trump voiced unity and inclusion.

Donald Trump knows how to communicate what he hates and despises. And he did so in his first inaugural address. At the very outside he targeted Washington, D.C., its insider politics and corrupt profiteering:

> For too long, a small group in our nation's capital has reaped the rewards of government while the people have borne the cost. Washington flourished, but the people did not share in its wealth. Politicians prospered, but the jobs left and the factories closed. The establishment protected itself, but not the citizens of our country. Their victories have not been your victories. Their triumphs have not been your triumphs. And while they celebrated in our nation's

capital, there was little to celebrate for struggling families all across our land.

President Trump also criticized the status quo of foreign aid, including military aid. He pointed out how our own military went underfunded while the United States funded other nations' militaries; he pointed out how we give trillions in foreign aid while our nation's infrastructure falls into disrepair and obsolescence. And in his own words, "We have defended other nation's borders while refusing to defend our own."

President Trump was elected to restore power from a corrupt political elite to the people, and he promised to do so. What matters, said President Trump, is that the people control their government and not the other way around. And the day had finally come for the people's president to take some action.

President Trump, like many others before him, promised to do a number of things in his first inaugural address. From day one it was going to be "America first."

President Trump promised the following action items:

- He promised to "bring back our borders"
- He promised to drain the swamp
- He promised to rebuild American infrastructure, making it the best in the world
- He promised to bring back jobs destroyed by foreign outsourcing
- He promised to get Americans off of welfare and back to work
- He promised only to sign trade deals that put America's interests first
- And he promised to erradicate completely Isalmic terrorism.

How well did he do? Shortly, we will take a look.

There were certain notable absences from President Trump's first inaugural address. First, despite having correctly identified what most Americans want from their government (great schools, safe neighborhoods and good jobs), President Trump only promised to protect U.S. borders and return outsourced jobs. He was silent on how to improve so many failing schools. He offered no plan to make more neighborhoods safer. In these three areas that mean so much to so many, President Trump offered so little.

How then can President Trump justify spending trillions more dollars per year? Whether it is for infrastructure repair or for military improvements, the proposed recipients of President Trump's rebuilding efforts are large, sophisticated and expensive. They are the opposite of the tens of millions who showed up to vote Donald Trump into office. In fact, they resemble creatures from the D.C. swamp President Trump promised to drain.

Personal Thoughts: President Obama and Chicago

I repeat my confession: I did not watch Donald Trump's inauguration. One reason, certainly, was that I was a little burned out from politics after waging my own campaign for more than half a year and losing. Campaigning required daily work and most days several hours were spent walking and meeting constituents in their homes. By January, I was exhausted and the Superbowl had not even taken place yet!

But there were other reasons. The big guy with orange hair just did not inspire me, really. Certainly not as strongly as then-Senator

Obama inspired me in 2008. The young junior senator from Illinois accomplished what no one before him had done - he was elected U.S. president before completing his first term of national office. Prior to that, no man had been elected president who did not already have a national reputation or a governorship.

Obviously, Barack Obama being an African American politician and succeeding to the presidency inspired all Black politicians in our country, myself included. He accomplished first what we all want to do - win the biggest prize out there.

Moreover, President Obama accomplished all of this by running a positive, hope-filled campaign. Rather than attacking or trying to bring down his opponents, he out-led them. He did this by aiming for the "better angels of our nature" and leading us. His main tools were phenomenal abstract political rhetoric (e.g., "hope" and "change"), leading by moral example (one wife, no affairs; two kids; Harvard Law, followed by community activism; regular church attendance), and deploying the well-oiled Chicago-based Democratic Party political machine.

Both Republican and Democratic Parties are not national organizations, even though each has a national committee. They are alliances of fifty separate state political parties, each with its own chairman or chairwoman, agenda, stable of candidates, and go-to issues. And skeletons. In order to rise to national prominence as a politician and candidate and, subsequently, office holder, one must secure the approval of the party bosses of his or her state or it will not happen.

Chicago, Illinois, is our country's third most populous city. Fittingly, this city had an all-American, meteoric rise just like its most famous presidential son. According to the 1850 U.S. census, Chicago had a population of less than 30,000. At that time it was smaller than my native Rochester, N.Y., by more than 6,000 people. It was dwarfed by the then-city of Brooklyn, N.Y., which had more than three times the population of Chicago. Chicago did not even rank in the top twenty U.S. cities.

Ten years later, Chicago had gained more than 82,000 net new residents. This catapulted the city into the top ten most populous cities in our nation. Recall that at this time the U.S. infant mortality rate was 181.3 and adult life expectancy was 39.4 years. Chicago has never looked back.

By 1870 Chicago's population had grown to almost 300,000 people, placing it in the top five most populous cities. *Chicago has never ranked lower since.* Only New York City has a greater claim to demographic dominance, but this was only possible because of a statistical quirk.

Chicago's Democratic Party was the Party of Obama: populous, industrial, unionized, working and middle class, multi-ethnic among Whites and multi-racial; a snapshot of the center left of American politics for the entire post World War II era. It was the party of both Chicago Mayors Richard Daley (father and son with a combined tenure of forty-three years in executive office), the party of the Reverend Jesse Jackson, the first African American to win a state presidential primary election. It is the party of former mayor Rahm Emmanuel. Chicago's Democratic Party has dominated Illinois politics forever and national Democratic politics since New York City lost its way in Democratic politics in the 1970s. This was one of Senator Barack Obama's greatest tools.

And finally, Barack Obama wrote books as a tool for national politics. He wrote (*not* ghost-wrote) a personal memoir of his family's unique American story up to the beginning of his career at Harvard Law School, and had it published at the start of his first failed Illinois state senate campaign. Then as a U.S. Senator, he published his second book, which became a N.Y. Times bestseller before Obama had completed his second year in office in that august body. And about three months later, Senator Obama announced his candidacy for the Democratic Party's nomination for the U.S. presidency. The rest is history.

Achievements and Set-Backs of Trump's First Administration

•••••••••●•••••••••

The remainder of this section is devoted to outlining the major achievements and set-backs of the first Trump Administration. I wish to avoid in depth analysis of the administration for a few reasons. First, it would be redundant. The events and circumstances of the Trump Administration have been the subject of news coverage - regardless of whichever coverage you have chosen, reader - since January 20, 2017. They will continue to be part of the news right on through Election Day 2020. There is no point in mechanically repeating facts or rehashing the opinions we are bombarded with everyday on Twitter. This book is not about news, after all. It is about what is *not* in the news, whether on CNN, Fox, MSNBC, ABC, CBS, the Daily Wire, Drudge, Hannity, Trevor Noah, et al. What is not in the news are the reasons why Donald Trump won the first time and why he will win again in 2020 - with or without the COVID-19 pandemic.

Second, I would find it boring. I am not CSPAN, and I do not regularly watch that channel. If I were reading this book, a play-by-play narrative of President Trump's first administration would cause me to close it.

Third, and most importantly, the day-to-day events and scandals leave little mark on America, on Donald Trump's presidency or on his likelihood of winning again in November 2020. Only certain events and decisions really count. The ones that count are representative of who Donald Trump is and what he stands for politically. Further, a particular event or decision does not even need to be the President's as long as he reacted to it publicly, characteristically, and irrevocably. That is how he puts his stamp on an event, position or idea, whether he intends to or not. Moreover, and this is the critical angle, the one that birthed the title of this book: the chief way to categorize these actions, events and reactions of President Trump is **disruption**. Donald Trump disrupted presidential campaigns as we know it. Now we will see how he disrupted presidential administration as we know it.

I will focus on seven events or decisions that show significant disruption of political, economic or moral status quo by President Trump. Each one could easily serve as the topic of a book in its own right. In fact, some of these books have already been written by others. No matter, we will discuss them here because what has not been done is to locate them within the narrative of longstanding discontent by the middle class, which gave birth to a disruptor, who got into office *to disrupt things*.

For a few moments, let us go even deeper. I said earlier that I am an evangelical Christian.

Reader, if you were to ask me, "Do you believe God Almighty wanted Donald Trump to win the Presidency?" I would say, "Yes." But not for the trite, facile, selfish, shortsighted, and hypocritical reasons I hear coming out of the mouths of my fellow mostly suburban, mostly White American evangelicals. After all, how many of them would hire a senior pastor who possesses no experience running a church, who has been married three times (and all of whose ex-wives remain alive), whose current wife is almost half his age, who has a potty mouth, who when challenged has almost no discernable relationship to truth, who characterizes immigrants from a neighboring country as murderers and rapists, who went on record saying he would *protect* the rights of homosexuals, who when asked if he donated money to Planned Parenthood, responded, "It's possible," who does not merely frequent casinos but owns them, who has never publicly described how he came to faith in Jesus Christ ... And the list goes on.

Not a chance! They would not hire him to run a small group! But we (yes) elected him President of the United States of America.

I believe Almighty God placed Donald Trump in the White House to disrupt every single institution in our society. Everything we take for granted, everything we draw comfort from in place of the Lord Himself, everything that makes us who we are as a nation, Donald Trump has disrupted or will disrupt. That is why he is there.

As we resurface - from above and not from below - reader, please note: not all of these events hold the same weight in my mind. The circumstances, President Trump's actions, and the import of the whole differs from case to case. The gravity of certain events and what their places are in the moral fabric of our nation cause deeper joy or pain, and have more lasting effects. These are the events I chose to write about.

Seven Events

●●●●●●●●●●●●●●●●●●●●●●

Repeal and Replace NAFTA

Throughout his first presidential campaign, Donald Trump promised to repeal or withdraw from "bad trade deals." From his first speech forward, Candidate Trump blasted these deals, claiming they were biased against America and American workers. He blamed stagnant wages of the U.S. middle class on bad trade deals. Further, Trump claimed the reason for higher unemployment among Blacks and Hispanics was in part due to job losses caused by bad trade deals.

The signature bad deal, according to Trump, was the North American Free Trade Agreement (NAFTA). NAFTA turned North America into one of the largest free trade zones in the world when it was enacted in the 1990's. The trilateral trade regime eliminated or reduced tariffs and other barriers to the movement of goods and services across the U.S.-Canada and U.S.-Mexico borders. Goods grown or manufactured in any of those three countries could be transported to and sold in one of the others with little interference. NAFTA also allowed for more investment opportunities between citizens and corporations of these three countries. Moreover, NAFTA created a common zone of protection for intellectual property rights.

Originally, the NAFTA treaty was signed by then President George H.W. Bush in 1991. However, the ratification process and two amendments lengthened the approval process. Once the whole package had been approved by Congress, then President Bill Clinton signed it into law. NAFTA took effect on January 1, 1994.

This, of course, led Donald Trump to blame Senator Hillary Clinton for NAFTA. After all, as First Lady she was part of the White House when President Bill Clinton signed it into law. To her credit, Senator Clinton established a record of pointing out some of NAFTA's problems and calling for it to be renegotiated. In fact, she did so during her 2008 presidential campaign against fellow Senator Barack Obama. But Obama struck first blood, claiming to United Auto Workers union members in Cleveland, Ohio, that Hillary Clinton supported NAFTA "until she became a presidential candidate."

The major reason repealing NAFTA had such power during the 2016 presidential campaign was that during eight years in office, President Barack Obama, who campaigned in 2008 stating NAFTA was a bad deal for American workers, did not change it. Then in comes billionaire real estate and media mogul Donald Trump in 2016, shouting out that NAFTA is a "bad, bad deal," and that he would repeal it.

Once in office, President Donald Trump continued to trash NAFTA and other "bad trade deals" and state that he would repeal them or withdraw. In May 2017, President Trump notified Congress that he intended to start negotiations with Mexico and Canada to replace NAFTA with a better agreement. By August 2017, U.S. and Mexican officials were already negotiating the new agreement. Canadian officials joined those talks later that year and the trilateral process quickly moved forward.

2018 proved to be the critical year for the United States-Mexico-Canada Agreement (U.S.MCA), which upon ratification by all three nations repealed and replaced NAFTA. Negotiations concluded successfully between the U.S. and Mexico first in August 2018; both nations signed the agreement. This immediately put pressure on the Canadians to join the regime. After one month they did. However, before the agreement could take effect, the national legislatures of all three countries needed to ratify it.

The Republican party had a major incentive for ratification to occur quickly: midterm elections were coming up in November. If the Republicans lost control of the House of Representatives and/or the U.S. Senate, this entire process might have been for nought. But ratification did not occur before Election Day 2018. Ironically, even though Republicans did lose control of the House as feared, this did not derail the nascent trade agreement.

Nancy Pelosi, longtime Democratic Congresswoman representative from San Francisco, was ushered back into the Speaker's chair. Now the Democrats had a seat at the negotiating table. They used it, but not in a way one would have expected.

Any student of current events over the past fifteen years would have expected Speaker Pelosi to fight against the new trade agreement. After all, Representative Nancy Pelosi voted in favor of NAFTA when it passed in the House of Representatives by a vote of 234-200 on November 17, 1993. (Then Democratic Congressman from Brooklyn, the Honorable Charles Schumer, voted against it.) In the intervening quarter century, you would have expected her to speak out against NAFTA if she thought it was a "bad, bad deal." In response to President Trump's announcement of his intent to negotiate a new agreement to replace NAFTA, Representative Pelosi stated, "Democrats have spent years fighting to rework NAFTA and other trade agreements to put America's working families first."

The fact that an untried Republican political candidate beat one of the most successful Democratc office holders ever is proof that no one believes Democrats have been fighting bad, bad trade deals. Instead, America's working families (and many other families) sided with Donald Trump.

And President Donald Trump got the job done. First, Mexico ratified the new agreement in June 2019. What followed was five months of negotiations over the concerns of Democrats in Congress about labor and environmental standards. These were successfully resolved, and the House of Representatives passed the USMCA bill on December 19, 2019. The U.S. Senate signed a similar bill on January 16, 2020. President Trump signed the act of Congress into law on January 29, 2020. USCMA took effect July 1, 2020.

This was a solid victory for President Trump. From campaign rhetoric to a completely new deal in place of America's most important trade agreement, Trump promised and he delivered. Moreover, this big picture, big vision type of deal is representative of why Trump was elected. Despite Representative Pelosi's rhetoric, the D.C. Swamp did not get it done. Bad trade deals persisted until Donald Trump took office. In spite of her claims, American workers and their families have come to rely on Donald Trump for better employment opportunities and fairer trade for Americans. And he delivers.

While this certainly was a victory for President Trump, Speaker Nancy Pelosi deserves credit, because there is one particular aspect of the process that, without her approval, would not have happened. Specifically, on December 18, 2019, the House passed two articles of impeachment against President Trump. If Speaker Pelosi had delayed a vote on USMCA pending the results of Trump's impeachment trial, it might not have become law at all. Hat tip to the opposition.

Repeal and Replace Obamacare

From the outset of his first presidential campaign Donald Trump set his sights on repealing and replacing the Affordable Care Act, more popularly known as "Obamacare," the signature domestic reform of his predecessor, President Barack Obama. Trump characterized Obamacare as "a total disaster" during his campaign. And he promised to repeal it "very, very quickly."

The Affordable Care Act was passed in 2010, when the Demoractic party held the majority in both the House of Representatives and the Senate. Otherwise, it would not have happened. This law mandated significant changes in how healthcare costs are apportioned among the four major players in the healthcare market: consumers, healthcare providers, insurers, and the government.

While the law is very complex (when passed it was more than 2,700 pages long; the total number of pages of regulations based on it is above 20,000 [sic]), the changes it imposed on U.S. healthcare can be summarized in eight key changes:

1) It eliminated the right of private insurance companies to deny insurance coverage to Americans younger than retirement age (65) who already had grave medical conditions when they applied for a policy.
2) The law extended the amount of time "children" may remain covered on their parents' private health insurance policies.

3) It reduced costs for seniors on Medicare by providing for free preventative care, including annual check-ups, and providing a subsidy for brand-name prescription costs for seniors who have reached the coverage gap.

4) It expanded eligibility for Medicaid (federally-subsidized state government health insurance based on lower income) up to 138% of the federal poverty line ($16,753.20 for an individual, $34,638 for a family of four in 2018).

5) The Individual Mandate, which required almost all American adults to obtain basic health insurance coverage or pay an annual penalty.

6) It provided tax credits for small businesses and other employers who pay for health insurance coverage for their employees.

7) It funneled billions of dollars annually into a fund to pay for lifestyle-change advertising (e.g., stop smoking; lose weight; etc.).

8) It eliminated both lifetime and annual policy coverage limits.

During his campaign, Donald Trump trashed Obamacare. As Election Day drew near, he was not the only one. In October 2016, former President Bill Clinton, whose political accume was clearly demonstrated by the way he navigated NAFTA through his first Congress in 1993, called the unsubsidized parts of Obamacare, "the craziest thing in the world." Clearly, there was widespread hostility to the law. President Clinton's comment makes one wonder how broad that hostility was.

What was the U.S. healthcare landscape like before Obamacare? Here are some key statistics: according to research done by the Kaiser Foundation, in 2010, there were 46.5 million uninsured Americans. This was approximately 17.8% of the U.S. population - nearly one person in five. Most of these people were adults. Most of them did not have pre-existing conditions preventing them from being insured at that time. Further, the age demographic with the greatest percentage of uninsured people was 20-30 year olds. Around 30 percent of persons in that age group did not have health insurance prior to Obamacare. However, according to the Centers for Disease Control, a federal government agency, the percentage of uninsured Americans had been steadily decreasing since 1998.

The most important statistics in my view, however, are not the percentage of American adults younger than retirement age who are without health insurance. The most important statistics relate to the collapse of a competitive health insurance market, which began roughly around 1999, resulting in skyrocketing levels of public health insurance coverage, and skyrocketing health care cost increases. First, the rate of private health insurance coverage has been decreasing since 1999. In that year, 68.3% of Americans younger than retirement age had private health insurance coverage provided through an employer. The total percentage of Americans with private health insurance coverage from whatever source in 1999 was 72.8%. This represents more than seven out of every ten Americans younger than retirement age. The total U.S. population under retirement age in that year was approximately 239.2 million people. So we are talking about 174.13 million people.

Meanwhile, in 1999, 21.5 million Americans younger than retirement age were on Medicaid. An additional 4.1 million Americans in this category were on Medicare (indicating that they were disabled).

One last statistic from 1999 completes the analysis: the total number of uninsured Americans younger than retirement age was 38.5 million. This constituted 16% of Americans younger than retirement age.

By 2010, the percentage of Americans younger than retirement age who were covered by private medical insurance had fallen to 56.3%. The population had climbed to approximately 309.3 million. Approximately 40.3 million people in 2010 were retirement age. Thus, this decrease in coverage among Americans younger than retirement age represents a net loss of private coverage by approximately 22.7 million people.

At the same time, the rate of public health insurance coverage skyrocketed. As mentioned above, according to the CDC, there were 21.5 million American adults younger than retirement age on Medicaid in 1999. By 2010 this number had increased to 27.6 million adults.

Basically, we (thanks to the corporate-controlled media) are focused on the wrong set of measures. The percentage of uninsured Americans had held relatively steadily from 1999 until 2010, when the Affordable Care Act became law. In the intervening ten years that percentage fell, only to begin rising again under President Trump. However, since most uninsured American adults younger than retirement age are between 20-39 years old and do not have pre-existing conditions, this statistic does not hold much water. It's just not that important.

Rather, the dramatic decline in employer-sponsored private health insurance coverage, the gobstopping rise of health insurance premium costs, and the skyrocketing levels of Medicaid coverage show us where the real problem is.

What's the verdict? Obamacare does not seem to be that bad. The numbers show that states have not gone bankrupt over increased Medicaid demands. The greatest success is the reduction in the percentage of people without medical insurance. That has been cut in half in ten years. Previously, it represented between 15-18% of Americans for decades.

The biggest failure, though, has been the inability to stop the constant rise in healthcare costs. The law does not address the real drivers: overconsolidation in the insurance market, reduction in the percentage of Amercans with employer sponsored private healthcare, and over subsidization of costs by the government. As in higher education, too much government money raises all prices.

Fighting the Opioid Crisis

One of the surprising, positive outcomes of the first Trump administration has been a significant reduction in the number of deaths caused by opiate abuse. By the time Donald Trump took office, our nation's opiate crisis was critical. Since 1999, according to the CDC, the number of natural opiate overdoses leading to death had *quadrupled.* By 2013, there were 44,000 opiate-induced deaths in America. The next year, the number rose to 47,000. But in 2016, 64,000 Americans died of opiate overdoses. This trend was both alarming and unsustainable. But things got worse.

Deaths from heroin overdoses skyrocketed from 2010-2015, increasing by more than 400%. Deaths from synthetic opiate (e.g., fentanyl) overdoses skyrocketed from 2013-2016 by more than 600%! Along with these increases in opiate overdoses our nation saw marked increases in both Hepatitis C infections and HIV infections. This is tragic, as the infection rates for both conditions had been on the decline for years. Between 1992-2009, the rate of Hep C infections had fallen by 87%. Between 2010-2016 it rose 167%!

More and more Americans were burning out and burning up because of opiate abuse, overdoses, and infections often linked to intravenous drug use like Hep C and HIV. Something drastic needed to be done to effect change before it was too late.

When President Trump took office in 2017, he took action on this issue. He declared a public health emergency about the opiate crisis in October 2017. This made available federal funds to combat this crisis.

The president did not act alone. Prior to his taking office, Congress and the Obama Administration had enacted multiple bills designed to address the opiate crisis. These include the twenty-first Century Cures Act, the Comprehensive Addiction and Recovery Act, Opiate Use Modernization Act, the National All Schedules Prescription Electronic Reporting Reauthorization Act, and others. Essentially, all of these bills do the same things. They provide money to federal or state government agencies or both. They also instruct federal agencies like the Food and Drug Administration, the Centers for Disease Control, or the Department of Health and Human Services to do certain things. Meanwhile, the death toll kept rising.

On the state level, legislatures began restricting the supply of prescription opiates that physicians may prescribe. Massachusetts was the first state to enact sweeping legislation that restricted the number of doses of prescribed opiates in circumstances of non-chronic pain, such as after a surgery. In March 2016, Massachusetts limited prescribed opiates for adults and children to a period of seven days. Further, this limit can only be exceeded in circumstances involving cancer treatment, chronic pain or palliative care. By September 2019, thirty-five other states had followed suit, limiting the number of days or doses of opiates that may be prescribed.

Significantly, more states with Republican-dominated adopted restrictions on opiate prescriptions than states run by Democrats.

Once President Trump took office, he began to work with Congress to enact legislation to stop and immediately reverse these trends in opiate overdoses. Within one year of President Trump declaring a national public health emergency on the opiate drug crisis, he signed into law the Substance Use-Disorder Prevention that Promotes Opioid Recovery and Treatment for Patients and Communities Act (SUPPORT Act). While this essentially did the same things as the previous barrage of federal legislation, there were some notable differences. First, the SUPPORT Act authorized far more money to treat opiate use disorder than the previous bills. Funds for treatment increased by $1.5 billion from 2017 to 2018. In fact, this constitutes the single largest federal appropriation in history to fight against a single class of drugs. Second, the SUPPORT Act authorized funds for the creation of Comprehensive Opiate Recovery Centers throughout the country. These programs and facilities, which include state agencies as well as nonprofits, provide a variety of services under this mandate, including medical care, housing, job training, counseling and other services. The status quo would have been to grant money to provide just one of those services and to one type of institution. Now under President Trump the old boundaries are being crossed. Third, the SUPPORT Act mandated that Medicaid provide new and improved services to fight the opioid crisis. As a result, the most economically disadvantaged addicts could access care *and* recovery services that not only would save their lives but help them return to a functioning, productive life.

The result? Between 2017 and 2018, the rate of overdose deaths decreased by 4.6%. The was the first decline in the rate for a *quarter century*. The decrease has been attributed to the significant decrease in both the frequency and the amount of prescription opiates made available to consumers.

By the following year, though, the rate shot up again, setting a new high. However, there was a silver lining. Prescription opiate-related deaths fell between 2018 and 2019, and continued to fall during 2019. Heroin-related deaths rose only slightly between 2018 and 2019, and fell during 2019. The increases in overdose deaths were mostly attributed to fentanyl and related synthetic opiates and to increasing cocaine use.

These are strong signs that President Trump's anti-opiate policy was working prior to the COIVD-19 disruption. Admittedly, the ground was laid by President Obama and the 114th Congress but the real push came under the Trump Administration.

Reshaping the Federal Judiciary

Early in his campaign, Candidate Donald Trump made very clear his intention to change the composition of the federal judiciary. "I am looking for judges and have actually picked twenty of them," he stated. "They'll respect the Second Amendment and what it stands for and what it represents." During many speeches in his campaign, Donald Trump promised to appoint federal judges who would respect the Constitution.

As of June 28, 2020, President Donald Trump has appointed and the U.S. Senate has confirmed 202 Article III judicial appointments. Under that provision of the U.S. Constitution, these appointments are for life with good behavior. As such, the power of appointment gives Trump the ability to influence U.S. law and policy for the next several decades.

President Trump's appointments include two Supreme Court justices (Gorsuch and Kavanagh), 53 appeals court judges, 145 federal district court judges, and 2 U.S. Court of International Trade judges.

How does this compare with Presidents Obama, Bush I and II, and Clinton? As of June 1st of the fourth year of a president's first term, Donald Trump leads all of them in total Article III judicial appointments. President Trump has appointed more court of appeals judges and district court judges by that point than any president in the past forty years. Further, at both the trial and appellate level of federal courts, President Trump's appointees make up *more than a quarter* of all judgeships. What is more, according to a report published by the Brookings Institute, the median age of President Trump's judicial appointees is 48.2 years old. This is almost a decade younger than the median age of President Obama's appointees (57.8) and lower than that of any president at *least* since JFK.

The significance of this achievement by President Trump can barely be stated in words. By using this power of appointment, Trump can remake the federal judiciary - the branch responsible for "stat[ing] what the law is," as the august Chief Justice John Marshall declared back in 1803. As a result, many of the battles of the "culture wars" will continue to be fought in the fora of the unelected branch of government rather than in the popular branch that actually is charged with making laws. That continues to represent a defeat for all those who support representative democracy as the only legitimate mechanism for creating the rules that govern a free society.

It is noteworthy, though, that thus far President Trump has only appointed two Supreme Court justices. This places him on par with his four immediate predecessors mentioned above, each of whom appointed two Supreme Court justices during their tenure in the White House. However, there is an ominous statistic in this context that should keep liberals up at night.

Two Republican predecessors of President Trump during the television age each appointed four Supreme Court justices to office, and succeeded in having them confirmed by the U.S. Senate. They were President Ronald Reagan and President Richard Nixon. Significantly, in each case, three of the four Supreme Court appointments were made during the president's *second* term. Moreover, in terms of total Supreme Court appointments, the tally of Presidents Nixon and Reagan can only be beaten before the advent of television.

As a lawyer who practices in federal courts, I feel obliged to add here a short note about Supreme Court Justice Brett Kavanaugh. The scurrilous, malicious, and dishonourable confirmation process Judge Kavanaguh was subjected to was without peer and without precedent in the annals of the U.S. Senate. Shame is the right word. Shame on the Senate Judiciary Committee and its unprincipled members who stopped at nothing in their attempts to thwart Judge Kavanaugh's confirmation.

What non-attorneys reading this book may not understand is that prior to his appointment to the U.S. Supreme Court by President Donald Trump in 2018, Judge Kavanaugh had a sterling legal reputation in our field. All major criticism of Judge Kavanaugh was directed at his politics rather than his legal abilities. Thus the American Bar Association (ABA) rated then Mr. Brett Kavanaugh "well-qualified" in 2003, when President George W. Bush appointed him to the D.C. Circuit Court of Appeals. Under political pressure, the ABA later downgraded Kavanugh's rating without a non-political basis.

The reality of the power of Judge Kavaugh's legal abilities continued to shine through once he was confirmed to the D.C. Circuit, a process which, by the way, took three years because of liberal political opposition to Kavanaugh's politics. While on the D.C. Circuit Court of Appeals, Judge Kavanaugh authored opinions in fourteen cases which were appealed to the Supreme Court. Thirteen times Judge Kavanaugh's opinions were adopted by the majority of the highest bench. This solidifies his reputation as one of the greatest appeals court judges in the contemporary area.

Ironically, perhaps, there is much to Justice Kavanaugh's life and background that resonates strongly with Democrats. Kavanaugh is as Irish Catholic as the Kennedys, with both sides of his family immigrating from Eireann to the east coast of the United States four generations ago. And thus began their rise. Both of Justice Kavanaugh's parents were lawyers; his mother was a judge before him, serving on the Maryland Circuit Court for Montgomery County. There is much to admire here in Kavanaugh's multi-generational story of hard-earned success, much that Democrats could rally behind. Alas, politics continues to get in the way.

China

As a businessman, Donald Trump has been on the record for decades criticizing government policies that affect American manufacturing. Specifically, he has criticized outsourcing.

From early in his campaign, Candidate Donald Trump threw down the gauntlet on trade with China. Trump regularly invoked the language of sexual violation to describe Chinese trade with America. At more than one campaign rally, Donald Trump would claim that "they're raping us." Trump also employed the language of theft to describe Chinese trade practices.

Despite the extreme rhetoric, other American political leaders held a critical view of Chinese trade practices. I am not referring to well-known intellectual property theft and other types of industrial espionage. I mean dumping, state subsidization, currency manipulation, and forced technology transfer. For some reason U.S. authorities always seemed to look the other way when it came to unfair trade with China.

Enter Donald Trump. Beginning in 2018, Trump began imposing a series of tariffs on goods imported to the U.S. regardless of source, like washing machines, but also specifically on certain goods coming from China. Naturally, the Chinese retaliated. The economic impact of these tariffs is measured in billions of dollars.

Generally I am against tariffs because they are inefficient economically. I prefer free trade and pursuing competitive advantage. When countries like China will not play fairly, I prefer closing the market to them entirely and negotiating bilateral treaties with critical partners who will trade fairly.

According to Industry Week, since China joined the World Trade Organization in 2000, the U.S.-China trade deficit in their favor grew to a total of $3.6 trillion by 2015.

How effective has President Donald Trump been in fighting for better trade with China? Most of the victory appears to be in the rhetoric. From 2018 when President Trump began his "trade war" with China through 2019, the trade deficit actually went down. That is the good news.

The bad news, as reported by CNN.com, is that it only went down 1.7%. Moreover, the total deficit was higher in 2019 than when the President took office in 2016.

Not exactly a hollow victory. But maybe this is the beginning of change.

North and South Korea

Of all the strange affairs that took place during the first Trump Administration the bizarre two-step President Trump has done with North Korean dictator Kim Jong-Un is hands down the most outlandish.

Arguably, North Korea is the most dangerous state on the earth. It is more dangerous than Iran, Afghanistan or even ISIS-controlled Syria. Possessing several nuclear weapons is only part of the reason, though it is obviously the most important. North Korea also has the largest standing army on earth, reputedly numbering three million men. Further, the number of decision makers within the North Korean power structure appears to be very, very small. Moreover, zero consideration is given to the mass of North Koreans who eke out an existence under Stalinist conditions.

How do I know all of this? After completing undergrad at Cornell University, I had the honor of living on the Korean peninsula. I spent two years teaching in a small Christian school in Seoul, the capital of South Korea. In fact, I was living there in 2002 when the North's regime kicked the U.N. inspectors out of the Yongbyon nuclear reactor facility, where uranium and possibly plutonium are enriched. I learned the language and grew to love that extremely industrious and intense nation.

Fast forward to 2016. North Korea has successfully developed and tested nuclear weapons. It has also tested multiple delivery rockets. Allegedly, North Korea possesses a rocket that could be used to strike the west coast of the United States.

Enter Candidate Donald Trump. He told a CBS TV show in February 2016 that he would "disappear" the North Korean dictator, who he called a "bad dude." Hardly the height of diplomacy. A few months later in May, Candidate Trump said he was willing to meet with Kim Jong-Un for face-to-face talks. Not only had there never been a meeting - or even a phone call - between the U.S. president and any of North Korea's grandfather-father-son dictator trio, but technically our two countries are still at war. While the suggestion may have been made off the cuff, it was literally without precedent in the annals of U.S. diplomacy.

Later that election year, North Korea successfully tested its largest nuclear device on record. The test caused an earthquake with 5.3 magnitude. Unfortunately, it was a harbinger of more bad news.

Once Donald Trump entered office, the situation between our two nations deteriorated rapidly. Kim Jong-Un boasted about his country's readiness to test an ICBM - the longest range nuclear armed rockets. Later that year North Korea successfully tested one, just like Mr. Kim said. Meanwhile, U.S. diplomatic efforts to bring global pressure on North Korea went nowhere. The U.S. and South Korean militaries conduct joint exercises only to be greeted by North Korea launching missiles. Then in September 2017 President Trump gave his first speech before the U.N. General Assembly in N.Y.C where he called the nuclear armed Stalinist head of state "rocket man," while threatening to "totally destroy" North Korea if necessary. Mr. Kim responded by calling the President of the United States a "mentally deranged U.S. dotard."

While it is hard to believe that what I am writing actually took place, because it is so childish, what is truly mind-blowing is that somehow within ten months both leaders would meet for a bilateral summit in Singapore. Seemingly out of the blue in January 2018, Mr. Kim began to speak about improving relations with South Korea. Within three months he issued an invitation to President Trump to discuss denuclearization. Security and logistical arrangements were set up over the next few months. All of these efforts culminated in a bilateral summit on June 11-12, 2018. For the first time in our history a U.S. president sat down with the head of a state against whom we were technically at war.

What did the summit accomplish? Many people have asked that question. There are several opinions available via the internet. I will leave that to them. What I want to point out is that President Trump did something that Presidents Clinton, Bush and Obama did not do. He changed the status quo and raised the stakes with North Korea by this summit gambit. He did not have to accept Kim's invitation. He could have just trusted the professionals, put his faith in one more round of sanctions, doubled down on isolation as a means to slow proliferation - a strategy that objectively failed in North Korea more than a decade ago. Instead, he took a risk. That's what leadership is.

Charlottesville, Virginia

My grandaddy was a Virginian. He was a tall, red-headed, gregarious, eloquent Black preacher who loved the Lord and loved his one wife and eight kids. Our family has lived in Virginia since the 17th century, which means that for our Black members, most of the time we were grappling with slavery and its implications. It was not pretty. It was evil.

On July 4th, a cousin of mine and I were on our way from upstate New York to Virginia for a family reunion. It was the annual gathering of my grandaddy's mother's clan, the Edwardses. We had just been introduced to them, because my granddaddy left Virginia for New York City in the 1940's. The next decade he would plant his branch of the family in free soil in the Genesee country, where I was born and raised without stigma. But the roots run south and run deep.

That early July morning we were driving down the Blue Ridge Mountains to Pittsylvania County. The sky was cerulean and the views took our breath away. I changed interstates from 81 to 64 to come eastward a little bit for a change of scenery. We stopped for gas on an exit off of I-64. The people were friendly in that charming southern way. Road signs near the interstate told us how many miles to Charlottesville, the home of U.S. Presidents Thomas Jefferson and James Monroe.

We turned south on Route 29 just before reaching the city. We were heading south again - further back and further in. But what if we had kept going into Charlottesville? Would we have reacted any differently to the hell that ascended there the next month? God knows.

Reader, you ought to be familiar with what transpired on Saturday, August 12, 2017, in Charlottesville, Virginia. Several groups of White supremacists had planned a rally to support keeping an equestrian statue of General Robert E. Lee. Thousands gathered to protest them and call for change. A twenty-year-old man drove a car into the protesters, killing a young woman named Heather Heyer. The man was from Ohio. The woman was born and raised in Charlottesville. Both are White. She had been active in supporting the Black Lives

Matter movement. Her last post on Facebook, allegedly, stated, "If you're not outraged, you're not paying attention."

Virginia governor Terry McAuliffe, a Democrat, was outraged at this recurrence of racist violence in his state. The following morning, a Sunday, he had the privilege of addressing his remarks to the congregation of the Mount Zion First African Baptist Church in Charlottesville. He directly confronted White supremacists with his words: "You go home, you stay out of here, because we are a commonwealth that sticks together." "You are not patriots." "You have made us stronger." Governor McAuliffe sought to persuade the Black congregation to give up its anger and to use hope. I do not know if he evoked the Lord Jesus in those efforts.

Governor McAuliffe also addressed the divisive political rhetoric of President Donald Trump. "We need to call it out for what it is. For the white supremacists and neo-Nazis who came to our beautiful state yesterday, there is no place for you here."

By now, reader, you know that President Donald Trump made three speeches about the tragic events at Charlottesville in August 2017. In his first speech he roundly condemned bigotry, hatred and violence and stated that it had no place in America. Here are the President's own words:

> But we're closely following the terrible events unfolding in Charlottesville, Virginia. *We condemn in the strongest possible terms this egregious display of hatred, bigotry and violence on many sides, on many sides.* It's been going on for a long time in our country. Not Donald Trump, not Barack Obama, this has been going on for a long, long time. It has no place in America. What is vital now is a swift

restoration of law and order and the protection of innocent lives. No citizen should ever fear for their safety and security in our society. And no child should ever be afraid to go outside and play or be with their parents and have a good time.

We love our flag. We're proud of our country. We're proud of who we are, so we want to get the situation straightened out in Charlottesville, and we want to study it. And we want to see what we're doing wrong as a country where things like this can happen. My administration is restoring the sacred bonds of loyalty between this nation and its citizens, but our citizens must also restore the bonds of trust and loyalty between one another. We must love each other, respect each other and cherish our history and our future together. *So important. We have to respect each other. Ideally, we have to love each other.* (Emphasis supplied.)

I actually caught the end of this speech live. I was impressed. The president's rhetoric was strong and evocative. After the shock of the events themselves, President Trump's words were reassuring.

The following morning, however, I learned that the liberal media were condemning Trump for his speech. They claimed his rhetoric was not strong enough. I laughed. These people all find something negative to say about President Trump. It never fails, I thought.

You see I did not hear the line I italicized above. If I had it might have given me pause the same way it did Trump's liberal critics.

For once, President Trump actually responded to calls from the Left that he needs to change. President Trump gave a speech the following day from the White House. Here is the central portion of his speech, followed by the peroration:

> As I said on Saturday, we condemn in the strongest possible terms this egregious display of bigotry, hatred, and violence. It has no place in America. And as I have said many times before, no matter the color of our skin, we all live under the same laws; we all salute the same great flag; and we are all made by the same almighty God. We must love each other, show affection for each other, and unite together in condemnation of hatred, bigotry, and violence. We must discover the bonds of love and loyalty that bring us together as Americans. Racism is evil, and those who cause violence in its name are criminals and thugs, including the KKK, neo-Nazis, white supremacists, and other hate groups that are repugnant to everything we hold dear as Americans. We are a nation founded on the truth that all of us are created equal. We are equal in the eyes of our creator, we are equal under the law, and we are equal under our constitution. Those who spread violence in the name of bigotry strike at the very core of America.
>
> …
>
> In times such as these, America has always shown its true character, responding to hate with love, division with unity, and violence with an unwavering resolve for justice. As a candidate, I promised to restore law and order to our country, and our federal law-enforcement agencies are following through on that

pledge. We will spare no resource in fighting so that every American child can grow up free from violence and fear. We will defend and protect the sacred rights of all Americans, and we will work together so that every citizen in this blessed land is free to follow their dreams in their hearts and to express the love and joy in their souls.

Thank you. God bless you, and God bless America.

The President was justly praised for these remarks. Further he had shown a sensitivity to the Left's perspective on race which, unfortunately, was not going to last forty-eight hours.

The following day at a press conference, President Trump fielded questions on several topics, including his remarks about the bloody events at Charlottesville. For the first time, the president addressed the tragedy off-script.

After praising the second speech he had given and talking about how everybody loved it, the president went on to explain what he had meant by his "both sides" comments. According to Trump, he had seen footage of persons on boths sides wielding homemade weapons. He thought both of those groups of people were bad. Further, he mentioned how there had been some people peacefully protesting the removal of General Lee's statue. The President claimed that these people were not neo-Nazis, although he also said, "I'm sure in that group there were some bad ones." Next, the President theorized about how far the removal of statues movement would go. "Are we going to take down statues to George Washington?" asked the sitting U.S. president, his forty-fourth successor. "How about Thomas Jefferson?" (The L.A. Times did an admirable job reporting all of this. The President's comments could still be found on their website in August 2020.)

What are we to make of this? For me, this was the president's lowest point in terms of my support for him. I understand if President Trump is trying to be the peacemaker between all Americans and bring together as many Amercans as he can under the same roof. But if President Trump actually believes his most high flown rhetoric, then he needs to pick a side and let the chips fall where God determines.

I will allow the father of Heather Heyer to have the last word on the darkest chapter in this book:

> "My thoughts with all of this stuff are that people need to stop hating and they need to forgive each other. I include myself in that forgiving the guy that did this. He doesn't know [any] better. I just think about what the Lord said on the cross. Lord, forgive them. They don't know what they're doing."

Amen, brother. I am sorry for your loss. You are correct. Forgiveness and redemption purchased by Jesus' blood on the cross are the only way out of this mess, y'all.

PART V

·············●·············

WHY TRUMP WILL WIN AGAIN

· · · · · · · ● ●· · · · · · · · ·

We seek no treasure, we seek no territorial gains, we seek only the right of man to be free; we seek his rights to worship his god, to lead his life in his own way, secure from persecution. As the humble labourer returned from his work when the day is done, and sees the smoke curling upward from his cottage home in the serene evening sky, we wish him to know that no rat-a-tat of the secret police upon his door will disturb his leisure or interrupt his rest.

> — Winston Churchill, speaking to U.S. Presidential Advisor Harry Hopkins in January 1941, attempting to persuade America to support Great Britain in her fight against Nazi Germany

Whither America?

At this point it should be very clear that we as a nation have lost our way. Our political leaders by and large lack a moral compass, do not live like us, the Middle Class, do not serve our interests, and do not intend to change. We face another momentous decision on November 3rd, 2020. Who do we want to lead our country and the free world? Before we decide, let us pause and take a reckoning of where we stand. Perhaps that will help us decide in which direction we wish to go.

After three years at the helm of the ship of state, President Donald Trump had built the strongest U.S. economy on record at any point in the last 150 years. Americans were experiencing rising incomes and rising savings. Unemployment was at historic lows and for African Americans and Hispanics at the lowest levels ever measured. Wall Street continued to post record high after record high. Thus, 401(k) balances were flush.

When Donald Trump took office in January 2017, there were an estimated 70,000 to 80,000 U.S. military personnel in the Middle East excluding Iraq and Afghanistan. Three years later the levels had remained basically the same, if not increased slightly. Thus President Trump can claim that he has not substantially increased U.S. military involvement in the most contentious region on Earth.

As regards China, the "trade war" instigated by President Trump's tariffs had yielded fruit. The U.S. trade deficit fell to $43.1 billion in November 2019, the lowest point since October 2016, placing the U.S. on the cusp of realizing its first annual decrease in the trade deficit since 2013. Further, imports of goods and services from China decreased for eleven of the twelve months in 2019. President Trump was on the cusp of delivering on his campaign promise to fight China and win.

A different reality set in in 2020. A new virus from China spread rapidly across the planet, killing tens of thousands of mostly older persons in the first three months of 2020. Then as the virus death rate accelerated during spring, the U.S. economy largely shut down due to the unconstitutional, unilateral actions of many state governors. Meanwhile, the murder of George Floyd, an African

American man, during his arrest for alleged trying to purchase a pack of cigarettes with a counterfeit $20 bill reignited spontaneous civil rights protests using the hashtag #BlackLivesMatter. Many groups standing up for equal rights for Black people were quickly infiltrated by anarchists, many of them White, who used the movement to cause wide-spread property destruction and mayhem in many American urban centers. A core downtown neighborhood of Portland, Oregon, was taken over by these terrorists for weeks with the local civil government proving powerless to stop them.

At the same time, calls for an immediate end to honorable recognition of Confederate Army leaders and veterans by state and local governments generated a shockingly swift response. Statues on public land were pulled down by government workers. In an even more symbolic victory, the State of Mississippi, once the bloodiest bastion of racist oppression in the land, unilaterally changed its state flag on July 1, 2020, removing the Stars and Bars from flying peacefully above, beside or inside many a state office building, courthouse and school room.

This is a year of upheaval. And somehow during all of this two men are running presidential election campaigns. One is the subject of this book. The other is former Vice President and former seven-term U.S. Senator Joseph R. Biden Jr, a consummate Washington D.C. insider and pillar in the Democratic Party. In spite of lockdowns, unlawful restrictions on public assembly and mobility, massive unemployment, and predictable civil unrest in U.S. urban centers, both men are publicly vying for the office that one of them currently holds.

At this point in the campaign (early August 2020), there have been no national party conventions, no television debates, none of the hallmarks of U.S. presidential election campaigns. Instead, stasis reigns. It has been a very hot, wet summer in upstate New York. But with shopping malls, casinos, churches and festivals largely closed since winter, not much is happening. Americans are stuck home waiting for something.

Arguably, the only circumstances that could be worse for President Donald Trump's reelection hopes would be if the U.S. were in the midst of a three-front war and losing with no end in sight. The political situation could not be worse for him and yet I fully expect him to win again.

I must confess I have believed President Donald Trump would win his reelection bid for at least the last year and a half. Despite COVID-19, partial economic collapse, colossal unemployment, and mass protests, I expect him to win again on November 3rd.

Reasons

The reasons are not simple but this final section of the book will present them. If you, reader, are willing (not capable, but willing) to remain objective, you will be able to understand the rational basis for my belief. If you will not remain objective, then more may be lost than your attention.

What is at stake, here, is the continuation of free, popular, representative government across the fattest, wealthiest, healthiest, most populous, and most fertile part *of the Western Hemisphere*. Whether we Americans stay free and united - that cardinal national virtue of our founding father George Washington - depends in large part on the outcome of the presidential election in November.

We Americans may not have been here before (in fact, we have faced down darker days four times). But two of our most important predecessors in Western Civilization have faced this same test. And they failed.

Both the Athenian *polis* and the Roman Republic were historic examples the American founding fathers and mothers specifically looked to when founding our republic. Their speeches were filled with quotations from Greek and Romand orators and statesmen. The publications and printed articles abounded with classical quotes and references. Their private correspondence was frequently referred back to the first republican government in world history and the heretofore greatest republic in world history.

Both the Athenian *polis* and the Roman Republic suffered similar, fundamental breakdowns in their governing and societal institutions as America has faced during the twenty-first century, which accelerated under President Donald Trump. Both the citizens of Athens and the citizens of Rome failed. The result in the first instance was the loss of the single virtue the Greeks prized first and foremost, which helped them discover that mankind was capable of creating and sustaining voluntary public order - namely, *sophrosuné* (self-governing freedom). Greek culture, trade savvy, exploration, and science would continue for centuries in Hellas, in Alexandria (the greatest Greek city that was never a state), throughout the Mediterranean basin and even as far away as Bactria, in Central Asia. Greek nationhood remained intact right into the modern era. But what good is being a nation if you cannot be free?

Rome's failure resulted in the swift enslavement of the entire Mediterrean basin - what was once called "the known world." The failure of free citizens possessing equal rights to discern, discuss and resolve *fundamental inequities of property and privilege, of opportunity and need*, within the system inherited from their fathers plunged the western world into an empire.

We Americans face that exact same challenge. We must not fail.

Reason One - Donald Trump is not a politician

When Donald Trump first ran for office, he claimed that politicians created our problems and, thus, could not be relied upon to fix them. It would take an outsider experienced with talking tough to politicians and getting his way. Someone who could think big and get things done. Someone who did not need to consult polls or get permission from the special interests first. Whether or not you, reader, think the above statements are true, most people living in most of America's counties agreed with them on Election Night in 2016 and voted for Donald Trump. I trust the same thing will happen on Election Night 2020.

Reason Two - Donald Trump gets things done.

To his credit, President Trump went out and got things done. Prior to the COVID-19 economic collapse, which was almost entirely caused by Democratic state governors, the United States was experiencing one of its biggest economic booms on record. Most American families were doing better in December 2019 than in December 2009 or December 2012. President Trump delivered on his promise to help Americans get safe neighborhoods and good jobs. He can take credit for that. Further, he took on China in the process. No D.C. insider or career politician would have dared to impose tariffs that might hurt American agriculture or manufacturing by making it harder to do business with China. Trump did. And the trade imbalance improved through November 2019. Once again, President Trump, who in day-to-day discourse does not always seem to check facts before he speaks or Tweets, did what he said he would do.

Now let us look for a moment at former Senator and former Vice President Joe Biden. Biden was first elected to political office in 1970 to county council in Delaware. He was first elected United States Senator - one of the most powerful offices in the world - in 1972. Since he transitioned directly from his Senate seat to the Vice Presidency, in effect V.P. Biden has been part of the Washington, D.C. Democratc Party establishment from 1973-2016, a period of longer than forty years.

Reader, ask yourself: can you name one thing V.P. Joe Biden accomplished during more than forty years in D.C. (more than thirty of which as a Senator)?

Reader, ask yourself: can you name one issue V.P. Biden has stood behind for at least ten years?

If nothing comes to mind, reader, ask yourself: what has V.P. Biden been doing in D.C. for more than forty years?

Soaking up the trappings of power, perhaps. Getting wealthier while more Americans got poorer, certainly. As a conservative Republican, I do not begrudge a man or woman making a fortune legally. But I do call into question how freely elected people become so wealthy while serving in public office. It is wrong. It is dangerous for our liberties and we must address it.

President Donald Trump got more things done in less than four years in D.C. than V.P. Joe Biden has done in more than forty. That alone is a reason to vote for a second Trump Administration. Moreover, it fits Trump's prescription that middle America's political problems are caused by career politicians like V.P. Joe Biden (in D.C., 1973-2016); Speaker Nancy Polosi (in D.C., 1987-2020); Senate Minority Leader Charles Schumer from New York (in D.C., 1993-2020).

On a personal note, I am a politician and proud of it. This is my vocation. I place much value on serving people in this manner. I fully recognize that for far too long we politicians have done a great disservice to our fellow American citizens. We cannot deny that. We owe the American people better. I look forward to being able to pick up our vocation from the cesspool it has fallen into, clean it up, purify it and put it back to work making Americans the most free and most safe nation on earth.

Reason Three - V.P. Joe Biden Will Not Choose the Running Mate He Needs to Win

I originally wrote this section in late June 2020, well before former Vice President Biden announced his choice of a running mate. I left it intact because it captures well my thoughts on how Biden thinks one step behind.

By choosing a Black woman running mate, Joe Biden gains nothing he does not already have and that will lose him the presidency. Why? Because that choice does not gain him any votes from other groups.

In 2016, with a White woman running for president and a White man as her VP, the Democratic candidate gained 94% of Black women's votes. Biden's choice demonstrates he has zero creativity, would prefer safe rather than risky bets, and confirms he is as tone deaf as every other member of the Democratic Party establishment. He also gives up the chance to gain something he does not have: a share of the third of Hispanic men, the quarter of Latinas, or 13% of Black men who voted for Donald Trump.

If you believe in racial politics how can you not see that by choosing a Hispanic man for VP, Biden would likely attract a sizable share of that voting block? With a Hispanic man as VP, Joe Biden wins Florida and the election. This should have been a no-brainer. Instead, a fatal misjudgment.

Reason Four - All Democratic Party Pundits Who Said The World Would End If Trump Was Elected Were Wrong

I am sorry, but did I miss World War III? Or did President Donald Trump choose not to blow Iran to kingdom come? Did he choose not to nuke North Korea? Did he choose not to use all of that new military spending to increase the number of troops in Iraq, Syria and Afghanistan? Did he choose not to start more drone wars?

Listening to those media pundits the last time, you would have thought we elected a madman. Instead, we elected a President committed to disengaging the U.S. military from places we should not be. That was the type of thing many *Democrats* said they wanted between 2004-2008. The opposite happened during the eight year Obama Administration. Did these Democrats change their minds? Or were they really just interested in frustrating the Republican agenda regardless of what that agenda was?

Reason Five - The Russian Collusion Allegations Were Unfounded, But That Did Not Stop the Democrats

For almost two years, former twelve-year FBI director Robert S. Mueller, III, investigated whether the Russian interference in the 2016 U.S. presidential election could be tied to Donald Trump and his campaign. The verdict? How about we quote from the Mueller Report: "the evidence was not sufficient to charge that any member of the Trump Campaign conspired with representatives of the Russia government to interfere in the 2016 election." (Mueller Report, p. 9.)

That should have been the end of the matter. I am not saying that Trump campaign officials who perjured themselves should have been left alone; they should have been prosecuted and several were. But as regards the President, the report concluded that there was no collusion. Congress should have moved on.

But they did not. The Democrats did a very bad job of hiding their intentions of trampling on the American people's rights by removing our constitutionally elected president. The Democrats in Congress wasted no time in undermining a report whose validity they would have defended to the death if Special Counsel Mueller had found evidence of collusion. First, the House Judiciary Committee, which has oversight over the Justice Department, including the FBI, called for former Special Counsel Mueller to testify about his findings. After his testimony did not yield any damning new evidence, the House Judiciary Committee sought to obtain evidence Mueller had uncovered through a "secret" grand jury proceeding but had chosen not to disclose in compliance with a federal procedural rule protecting the secrecy of grand jury testimony. Initially, the House committee asked the Department of Justice for the grand jury testimony. When Justice refused, the House Judiciary Committee took them to court over the matter. Their petition was available online at the time of this writing at: https://www.politico.com/f/?id=0000016c-2fe0-d88f-a9ec-2ffd669a0001.

At the back of this memorandum, in the section entitled Prayer for Relief, the House Judiciary Committee laid bare its rationale. The secret evidence was necessary to determine (1) what President Trump knew about the Russian election interference; (2) if the

President knew of any contacts, whether formal or informal, between his campaign and Russia; (3) if the President knew of any potential criminal acts by him, by his administration, by his campaign, by any staffer or other contact in his administration or in his campaign or by anyone he knows; (4) what actions President Trump's former White House Counsel McGahn took during the campaign, the transition and during his service in the administration.

In other words, in spite of the fact that an excellent lawyer with a flawless record as director of America's top counterintelligence agency for twelve years told the House Judiciary Committee and the whole world that there was no evidence of collusion between President Trump, his campaign, and the Russian government, and in spite of hours of personal testimony by former Special Counsel Mueller before the committee, the Committee still needed to see this evidence to determine if what Mr. Mueller and his report said was true.

Respectfully, this was disingenuous. The truth is that it was a witch hunt. The House Judiciary Committee would only accept one answer and its corollary: Donald Trump colluded with Russia to win an election he would have lost without their help and, thus, the constitutional result of Election Night 2016 was illegitimate. Whenever someone told them otherwise, they just refused to believe it.

The House Judiciary Committee was successful in getting a federal judge to authorize release of the grand jury evidence. The Department of Justice appealed, and the judge's decision was upheld by a divided appeals panel. Critically, D.O.J. appealed the dispute to the Supreme Court, who agreed to take this case. This means it is unlikely the House Judiciary Committee, even if they prevail, will be granted access to this evidence before the November 2020 presidential election.

No matter. I don't mean that cynically or spitefully. What I am referring to is the fact that the House Judiciary Committee has been saying the same thing since early 2017: we need to find out if Donald Trump and his campaign colluded with Russia to win the election. They are never going to stop. This is not going to go away until the Democrats lose their majority in the House of Representatives, and that could occur this November.

Reason Six - Democratic Governors Jumped the Gun On COVID-19 and Needlessly Destroyed the American Economy

New York is by-far the state hit hardest by the coronavirus. At the time I am writing this, we still have more than twice as many deaths as the number two state, New Jersey.

With that being said, no essential business in N.Y. has had even a quarter of its workers test positive for the novel coronavirus, let alone experienced a fatality rate of at least 2%. Even nursing homes, the business in N.Y. with the greatest predictable fatality rate from COVID-19, has not experienced a 10% infection rate among its workers - employees, consultants, and contractors.

Arguably, if nonessential businesses had followed the same protocols - the *minimum* are wearing masks, washing hands, and social distancing - they would have experienced the same level of infections and deaths.

Thus, the widespread shutdown of the United States economy in early spring 2020 at the hands of New York Governor Andrew

Cuomo, California Governor Gavin Newsom, Pennsylvania Governor Tom Wolf, Illinois Governor JB Pritzker, Ohio Governor Mike DeWine, North Carolina Governor Roy Cooper, and Michigan Governor Gretchen Whitmer, was largely unnecessary. Millions of jobs lost, millions of small businesses destroyed, when a more deliberate response that left control in the hands of business owners would have likely achieved similar results against the spread and lethality of the novel coronavirus without destroying our economy.

Please note: the governors mentioned above are all Democrats, save one.

If you believe the shutdown was premature, unnecessarily widespread, too long and unconstitutional, then please vote Republican in November 2020. Remember that this year a handful of men and one woman shut down the most powerful economy on earth over a virus that *outside of nursing homes killed less people than the flu*. The shutdown should never have happened.

Ignore the protests. Ignore the smoke and mirrors. Refuse to be baited by the sideshow bologna. Turn off your television - that's how the left wing media reaches you. And on November 3rd, 2020, show up at your polling place with a mask on, a spare mask for a "forgetful" friend, and a heart that does not waver when our freedoms are threatened.

I am not fooled by the Left. Violence is what they condone. Violence is what they will do. What are they after? Your freedom. They want to take away your right to live how you want to. Because they hate it. Because it scares them. Because they would do things differently. And they will use any means necessary to do it.

Reason Seven - More Americans in More Places Want Our Government to Set People Free Rather Than Tell People How to Live

Ultimately and most deeply, we American voters must question what purpose we wish our government to fulfill. It is our greatest privilege. There are only two choices, which fits the binary nature of the American character. Americans are accustomed to choosing between only two alternatives, unlike several other Western nations - let alone nations scattered across the globe. For us, it is either football or baseball, pizza or hamburgers, rock and roll or hip hop, black or white, Democrat or Republican. This is how we have been hardwired to make choices.

Here they are: either we want our government to set people free or we want our government to make people better. Those are the only two choices.

To set people free is the raison d'etre of the United States of America. It is why we exist as a country. The free nation that inhabits the country was produced when persons from all corners of the globe came together under one Constitution and a set of common laws in North America. There has likely never been an adult who *voluntarily* came to our shores who did not dream of being free. Unfortunately and for far, far too long, many of those immigrants found a harsh and bitter reality waiting for them in the Land of the Free. But - *but* - they did not leave. They did not return to the oppressed lands from which they had fled. Instead, they gritted their teeth, and worked. They narrowed their gazes and stared down their new oppressors. They joined hands and marched upward to justice and equality. Not right away. But certainly over time. Their children, grandchildren, great-grandchildren and great-great grandchildren stood up for their freedom. Many marched for their freedom and the freedom of others. Many continue to march today.

This March of Freedom is the great existential work of the United States. It is mostly performed within our continent rather than elsewhere in the world. Our greatest battles, *defeats* and victories have been on this continent: against the native nations who got here first; against the African nations whose members we enslaved; against ourselves; against our brothers and sisters, cousins and neighbors; against strangers from across the border. We struggle to learn to live *together* and not just side by side. This is what it means to be free *and* equal.

Free and Equal. This is what it means to be American.

These qualities are co-dependent, though it might not seem that way on the surface. When we plumb the depths of history, the true nature of these values is revealed. Thus whenever we see a Western society that purports to be free but continues to tolerate slavery and systemic injustice against an objective human "Other" within that society, eventually that society loses its freedom or is expelled to another place. In a certain sense, this is a just outcome. How can a man cherish, *hallow*, freedom but deny it to another?

Choosing to set others free achieves the opposite effect. Both fifth century Athens and the Roman Republic were free and strong for centuries before Christ in large part because each society used existing institutions to integrate the Other into the franchise. Or, they created new institutions to transform new men into new citizens. In neither case was the work completed, nor was it perfect, but this was the direction in which freedom led those ancient citizens.

This analysis also shows powerfully the necessary role government institutions play in this work of setting people free (equal). Athenian society was the first human society within the historical period to achieve both political (no king or hereditary ruler) and personal (individual) freedom. The narrow road which led the Athenians from despotism to freedom necessarily involved confronting and solving fundamental social, economic and political problems that all post-tribal societies face.

All post-tribal societies are concentrations of unrelated families sharing a common location, language and laws, identity and institutions. All post-tribal societies have an agrarian economic base. All post-tribal societies manufacture and trade goods with other societies, recognizing thereby an internal inability to produce everything they need and want for daily life, and trusting in other societies to work, produce, create and sell affordably other vital products. All post-tribal societies share a common religion or rituals. And until the Athenians came along, all post-tribal societies had a single government - usually by king, sometimes by an oligarchy.

The Athenians fundamentally changed the structure and purpose of their government and their society by confronting and solving the problems of the poor and disenfranchised. Sic. It was certainly by an act of divine guidance that Athens produced, educated, and equipped the first statesman in western history: Solon. Although a landed aristocrat, Solon was a merchant before he entered the political arena. Successful trade brought him wide contacts throughout the eastern Mediterranean Sea, which brought him into contact with a variety of Greeks as well as with non-Greek civilizations to the east and south. An accomplished poet, Solon had a practiced gift with words. Part of his political genius was using this ability to persuade his fellow citizens to fundamentally restructure their society to make it more fair and thus more stable.

Briefly, Solon reformed the Athenian constitution and Athenian society by placing them on more moderate grounds; all sides gained something; no side lost everything. Solon's major reforms can be divided into four categories: individual rights and duties; political enfranchisement; legal and judicial reforms; and social and economic restructuring. Solon's stated aim was to expand the political and economic power of the free common man and to inspire all of his fellow citizens to relate to each other in *eunomia* (harmonious public order characterized by restraint).

On individual rights and duties, Solon abolished slavery for debt and set free those citizens *and their family members* who had been made slaves through this barbaric practice. Farms taken from these former debtors or farms encumbered by these obligations were restored to their rightful owners. Solon introduced testamentary dispositions of property after death (wills), allowing family property to pass with less interference. Solon regulated marriages, preventing old men from offering themselves for "adoption" to families without male heirs so as to marry a wealthy virgin and steal her property. On the duty side, Solon passed a law commanding all citizens to teach their sons how to read. He passed a law requiring fathers to instruct their sons in their own trade. Thus, under Solon's reforms, each succeeding generation of citizens stood on its own feet as an educated body and a skilled workforce. This was a truly radical innovation, though, because most of the citizens were neither wealthy nor middle class. Solon had effected a social revolution by legislation and avoided civil war.

On social and economic restructuring, Solon organized Athenian society into four classes based on wealth: *pentakosiomedimnoi* (the 500 Bushel Men), *hippeis* (the Horsemen or Knights), *zeugitai* (the Oxen Men) and *thetes* (the Free Peasants). This radically transformed Athenian society, because it was based on economic circumstances rather than on blood or marriage. All four social classes had the same economic and judicial rights, but not the same political rights. Citizens of all four classes exercised the political franchise - all citizens could vote and hold office. But they did not have the same privileges and duties.

The 500 Bushel Men paid the most taxes; they alone had the right to sponsor public games; they alone had the right to stand for the archonships (nine), which were roughly the Athenian equivalent of Roman counsels; Athenian archons were members for life in a deliberative body called the Areopagus. However, through Solon's reforms, the Horsemen quickly acquired the right to stand for the archonships. They acquired their name from their ability to supply their own horses during war.

The middle rank was taken up by the Oxen Men, who were mostly landowning small farmers. Through this reform, they were empowered to serve in all offices of the state except the archonships. Further, they apparently gained the right to sit on a new council called the Boule, which helped counterbalance the influence of the Areopagus.

On legal and judicial reforms, Solon granted a right to prosecute to all Athenian citizens; he granted to all Athenian citizens a right to appeal decisions by government officers to the Ekkleisa, the great body of their fellow citizens; he further institutionalized the prohibition against vendettas, ensuring that the state alone sought redress for murder.

All of the Athenians' future achievements, their tremendous accomplishments in philosophy and natural science, mathematics and art, rhetoric and military arts, all were made possible because one man set them free. This is statesmanship par excellence. This is an excellent example of one of the two purposes of government.

One last note on Solon: despite many offers, Solon refused to accept the dictatorship of Athens. He was elected. He used persuasion to move his fellow citizens to change their reality to make it more fair and more sustainable. Then he retired and left the stage leaving the free world ever after in his debt.

The other choice for what a government should do is to make people better. Now to *inspire* people to *behave* better is the aim of all true works of justice. Whether in the home or in the marketplace, in the courthouse or in city hall, in church or synagogue or mosque or temple, the purpose behind all genuine movements of justice is to encourage people to behave better. We are all familiar with the Golden Rule. But how many of us *do* it?

Both Mohandas K. Gandhi and the Reverend Doctor Martin Luther King, Jr., shared the moral conviction that the violence of the fascist oppressors against whom they were engaged in battle (the British colonial government in India and the racist, unconstitutional White supremacy institution governing the U.S. South) could not - *could not* - be used against them to achieve a *moral* as well as a material victory. Instead both men preached nonviolent resistance to oppression as a means to provoke men to behave better. A major factor in the success of each of these great prophets of change, for that is what they were, is that each pursued specific, measurable, attainable goals, rather than vague aims or platitudinous normatives. Mr. Gandhi wanted national independence for India. Another way of putting it was, get the British out and we govern ourselves. Dr. King's immortal Dream was reached through very mortal steps and stages: equal civil rights, equal political rights, equal economic rights. Then the Dream would be possible. Without these preliminary and intermediate goals, the Dream would be a mocking fantasy. Mocking, because this struggle to be free and equal takes place in the Land of the Free.

Reader, please note: each of these movements was private, self-funded and voluntary. *All true movements of change by mankind are so.* When considering the fundamental purpose of government, however, we confront a different type of problem.

The other choice of a government's purpose is to make people better. Politically speaking, this is the root of all kinds of evil. There are four fatal presuppositions underlying this distorted aim. First, there is something wrong with each citizen - for each citizen will be bound ostensibly by the government's rules. Second, it is possible for mankind to improve through temporal and material means. Third, government (the legislative, regulatory, enforcement and judicial processes only) is capable of fixing that which is wrong with each citizen. Fourth, government has the authority (i.e., the legitimate power) to compel individuals to live in the way it chooses.

Did you notice what is missing? The political element is missing. The political element is elective: the citizens choosing their leaders. In the West, this is the only legitimate basis for a government's authority. In all regimes that adopt the second choice of a government's fundamental purpose, the political element is first undermined, then it is marginalized, abandoned, and forgotten.

Choosing this second aim grants the government permission to take free society into slavery - slavery to the Government. Partisans of this choice label the direction in which they are pushing society Progress, but this is propaganda. These partisans deliberately obscure the truth about what they are after until it is too late. And what are they after? They want to make you think and act the way they want you to think and act. Their means of achieving this is the use of a totalitarian government. The moment it is too late is when a free man or woman no longer has a choice but to do what the government says.

The Road to Political Slavery

What are the sign posts and mile-markers as it were, of this road? For the sake of clarity and brevity, I will limit myself to the six major markers. Step One is taken when citizens voluntarily give up their rights in a certain domain to the government. Take for example, the education of children. Each family has a moral duty to educate its children. It is right for the government to make this duty imperative under law. In doing so, it is wise for the government to create institutions of education and fund them with tax dollars. No reasonable citizen objects to this.

Loss of Choice

The point of departure down the Road to Slavery in this regard is the loss of choice. Or, more accurately, the surrender of control. When only the government's educational institutions may be used by the citizens to fulfill this duty, there has been a loss of control. When local society can no longer determine what is taught, there has been a loss of control. Once the government can force you to send your kids only to its schools and it controls what is taught, this process should no longer be called education. It is indoctrination. The bureaucrats know this. It is their stated aim.

Recall that in late April 2020 - during the height of the coronavirus pandemic in the northeastern United States, when almost all school systems were shut down to in-person learning and millions of American families were grappling with the unanticipated burden of remote home education, Harvard Law School Professor Elizabeth Bartholet called for a nationwide ban on homeschooling. Her stated rationale is best left to her own words:

> The issue is, do we think that parents should have 24/7, essentially authoritarian control over their children from ages zero to 18? I think that's dangerous. *I think it's always dangerous to put powerful people in charge of the powerless, and to give the powerful ones total authority.*
> (Italics added)

My friends, that is exactly what totalitarian governments do. Thankfully, Professor Bartholet was clear in her motives; it makes it easier to fight back and defend our rights. Moreover, this is only one example of many in our society today of powerful persons pushing America in the direction of Total State Power. Please remember that not all of them speak from the Left.

Collapse of Competitive Politics

Step Two on the Road to Slavery is the collapse of competitive politics. In order for politics to be competitive, two things must occur. There must be at least two, strong political parties upholding different political principles and pursuing different goals, whose candidates contest elections that either candidate has a reasonable chance of winning; and there must be regular turnover of office holders exercising power. En bref, a different party in power on some kind of a regular basis and different people in office.

From our bloody birth in 1776 until the twentieth century began, competitive politics were part of the spirit of America. As the famed British political scientist John Stuart Mill would say in his masterwork, *On Liberty,* "A party of order or stability, and a party of progress or reform, are both necessary elements of a healthy state of political life." But there was no organized political opposition to the party in power until 1792.

From 1789 until 1792, there was a unity government under President George Washington. This fit both Washington's national vision and political principles. Underneath him, though, a nascent political party structure was operating. They soon became known as the Federalist Party.

Washington's first Secretary of State, fellow Virginian Thomas Jefferson, held different political principles. Jefferson was a political genius; he knew that his different political principles demanded he oppose the Federalist agenda and that such opposition required an organized political party. So, he resigned from the national government to build it with the help of his longtime friend and political ally, fellow Virginian James Madison, Jr. Within four years, Jefferson and Madison succeeded in organizing a political party popular enough and strong enough that Jefferson lost the 1796 presidential election by only eight electoral votes in a four-way contest.

Ever after, the United States presidency has been fought for by at least two strong political parties. In 1801, Thomas Jefferson succeeded in winning the first of two terms as president. He was the first Democrat in that office. From that year until roughly 1901, the two party system worked well. Organized, successful political opposition led to frequent changes in power in the Executive Branch. It also led to the creation of two new political parties that succeeded in placing a man in the White House: the Whig Party (Presidents William Henry Harrison, Tyler, Taylor, and Fillmore); and the Repubican Party (Presidents Abraham Lincoln, Grant, Hayes, Garfield, Arthur, Benjamin Harrison, and McKinley). Further both the Democratic Party under Presidents Andrew Jackson and native Dutch speaking Martin Van Buren, and the Republican Party under President Abraham Lincoln and his successors reached their modern stage of development in terms of political principles: the Democrats supporting the common man and local institutions; the GOP supporting big business and other national institutions.

The twentieth century dawned for the American people on September 14th, 1901. On that day in Buffalo, New York, President William McKinley died, completing the assassination begun on September 5th, when an anarchist shot him twice in the abdomen. Vice President Theodore Roosevelt, Jr., the 42-year-old scion of one of New York's oldest and wealthiest families, was sworn into the highest office in the land. He had barely been vice president for six months. It was his first national office.

President Teddy Roosevelt, the youngest man to serve as Chief Executive, would do much to bring America quickly and strongly into the new century. But that is not what we need to discuss here. We need to discuss how the demographics of national party politics changed from that point onward.

From that point onward no new political party was organized strongly enough to succeed in placing a candidate in the White House. Further, the Democratic and Republican Parties both went through significant changes in membership and political principles. Whereas before a new political party organized around new political principles would have been established by a group of concerned, well-financed citizens, now both of the two national parties simply absorbed new and sometimes contradictory principles. They also absorbed new members who brought with them different political principles. For example, the Democratic Party, longtime champion of the common man and local institutions, became the party (outside of the South before roughly 1970) that fought for equal rights for African Americans, our country's oldest, internal racial Other. Later on they became the party fighting for increases in national and state regulation, necessarily accompanied with increases in government payrolls. Thus the twenty-first century Democratic Party has been pushing a so-called environmentalist initiative that many see clearly as a regulatory power grab.

On the other side of the aisle, the GOP, whose main geographic powerbase was in the North and the West, with small pockets of Black support in the South post-Reconstruction, started adding scores of White Southerners fleeing the pro-Civil Rights Democratic Party in the 1960's and 1970's. This made it difficult for the GOP to sustain its role as the champion of equal constitutional rights for all Americans, because Southern Whites had been explicitly opposing that political principle for generations. Further, the GOP acquired a sudden sight for the common man and his *local* problems and challenges. GOP candidates and officeholders began speaking about lower taxes not only as a means to increase profits for businesses and individuals, but as a means of achieving smaller government.

Certainly democratic (small D) politics makes strange bedfellows. But the losers in this twentieth century exchange have been American voters. Rather than being empowered to choose between a common man party, a big business party, a pro-environment party and a small government party, voters have only two choices. In the short run, we end up with some of each and all of none. When we take the long view, we see that what we have really done is empowered the elites who run these two parties to decide for us what matters and what does not. This is a loss of freedom.

Realising that both the Democratic and Republican leadership elites are the only winners in our political system serves as a good transition to the second element of Step Two: over time, politicians have been staying longer and longer in office. As a direct result, there are fewer and fewer office holders at the national and state levels. Fewer and fewer people are deciding what should be prohibited and what should be permitted.

When Theodore Roosevelt became president, the average age of a member of the House of Representatives was under 50 years old. Currently, the average age of a member of the House of Representatives is 57.6 years old. This represents a gain of about ten years since President Teddy Roosevelt's day. While ten years might not seem like that much, the average tenure for existing members of the House more than doubled between 1900 and 2016. Thus, we see fewer persons exercising political power, starting later and staying longer.

The coup de grace, however, is the increase in average income of our national elected officials. Admittedly, it is hard to measure. Apparently, the government and/or other institutions did not begin keeping track until around 2004. Perhaps they thought it was not important. Meanwhile, Malcolm Forbes began publishing his tally of the 400 richest Americans in 1982.

Between 2004 and 2016, the median Congressional income rose from around $800,000 to well over $1 million. Moreover, since 2012 most members have been millionaires. At the same time, as I discussed much earlier in this book, most middle class families got poorer between 1990 and 2015. According to Money Nation, from 2007 to 2015, the average net worth of the American family dropped from $126,000 to $77,000. During that same timeframe, the networth of the *average* Congressman or Congresswoman grew 20%!

Before we move on to Step Three, I feel compelled to point out who sits at the top of this heap of corruption, for that is what it is. Even U.S. Senators, whose median income easily dwarfs that of their colleagues in the House of Representatives, do not make even $200,000 per year. On top of that, the U.S. Constitution prohibits a sitting Congress from voting an increase in its own compensation. Obviously to no avail.

Who sits at the top? You can google it, right? Try.

In sum, fewer and fewer Americans get into office. Those who get in started older and they stay longer. And they are rich beyond the dreams of their fellow citizens. Ask yourself: what is the likelihood that they will even understand your circumstances, let alone protect your rights?

The Militarization of Civil Society

This step involves much more than what has happened since the United States military began giving military weapons, including armored vehicles, to state and local police departments in the 1970's, to be unleashed *against their fellow citizens* resisting arrest, in circumstances without legal or judicial accountability for misuse of power, disproportionate response, lack of probable cause or other legal principles that protect a free society. This step, in essence, concerns everything that follows when the security apparatus of the state, which is an essential part of government, turns its gaze from outward-looking to inward-looking. Once citizens become the subjects of widespread suspicion by persons in authority, they then become the targets of widespread monitoring, interdiction and destruction.

A friend of mine who was born in the generation before me has a theory about freedom in the United States that shocked me when I first heard it, but, as time goes on, makes more and more sense. He believes freedom for Americans peaked in about 1970. At that point, the Civil Rights movement had achieved all the successes it would in that generation. Americans could go where they wanted, do what they wanted and live how they wanted. I am tempted to label this the California Effect, but I will resist; there is certainly some of Nevada in this. And N.Y.C. And other parts of our great culture. And California has changed for the worse.

In terms of images, think of the happy, healthy middle class family: two cars, two incomes, suburban; the children will go to college (affordably); the house will appreciate; the interest rate on savings is so high it obviates the need for personal investing; more and more comforts have entered the market; etc., etc. This is freedom. The obverse is a longhaired eighteen-year old pushing his convertible over the speed limit without a seat belt, a beer in one hand, the other hand squeezing the shoulder of his sixteen-year-old bikini-clad girlfriend while she tokes beside him. His twelve-year-old brother lays down in the backseat, dreaming of being in the driver's seat. This is also freedom.

Then somewhere between 1970-1974, the counterrevolution began. It was largely regulatory at both the federal and state levels. Agencies and bureaucrats began publishing numerous regulations prohibiting a whole host of activities that ten years before few people would have accepted as subject to government regulation.

The agencies and bureaucrats have not stopped and now our society is caught in a spiderweb of red tape.

Congress and the state legislatures also played their role. All of the big picture prohibitions came by legislation. As time went on, legislation became longer, less coherent, and more invasive.

Please note: it is important to remember that the rationale behind much of this regulation is benevolent. For example, mandating seat belt wearing. The state legislators who passed those laws and the bureaucrats who wrote those regulations were trying to save lives. More than any other automobile innovation or technical development, and more than any other regulation, this one change has saved more lives of Americans involved in automobile accidents. But it still involves a loss of freedom by Americans.

So why am I talking about seat belts in a section about the militarization of civil society? Because the next step for the government after prohibiting certain activity is to enforce its own rules. More rules means more enforcement, which means more monitoring and interdiction. Further, more invasive rules (e.g., rules against possession of naturally-growing substances, rules against certain types of relationships, rules about how certain services like restaurant food must be provided) means more invasive monitoring.

However, there is another problem besides loss of freedom that ubiquitous, exhaustive regulations created. It has conditioned the American people to look to governing authority for permission about what to do and how. It is conditioning us to follow orders.

Now let us examine key elements of the militarization of police in the United States and in Great Britain. When our country was founded in 1776, there was no police force in any of the thirteen colonies. Nor was there a police force anywhere in England. Law and order were kept in both places by justices of the peace and constables, Anglo-Saxon institutions of local public order with roots died deeply in the woad. They were charged with keeping the king's peace: no murder, rape, robbery, theft, riot, poaching. Additionally, sheriffs - or shire reeves, served similar ends. These were officers appointed by the king who were responsible for executing the king's writs or judgments in a given area of Britain. When the Normans conquered England, their kings changed the names of the reeves to bailiffs.

Reader, you may recall that one of the causes of the revolt in Massachusetts during the 1770's was the obnoxious presence of British troops in and around Boston. Their presence in several of the colonies was due to the French and Indian War, which Britain had won in 1763. Prior to that war, there was no widespread presence of permanent organized military units in any colony. Various acts of Parliament, beginning with the Mutiny Act of 1765, ordered all of the colonial assemblies to provide lodging for British troops. The assemblies were reluctant to do so. Over time, Parliament provided more and more specific orders about what type of establishments could be forced to house British troops. The situation deteriorated so rapidly that within eleven years the colonies declared independence.

What was the problem with housing troops ostensibly in the neighborhood, as it were, for one's protection? The rights of Englishmen. "No taxation without representation" - a slogan from Massachusetts following the 1773 Boston Tea Party - was not the only constitutional right the English-speaking colonists claimed. The right to be secure in one's property without *unwarranted* - meaning without a judge-issued warrant supported by probable cause - intrusion was another. The problem of quartering British troops in American buildings was so important that it was referred to explicitly in the Declaration of Independence:

> He has combined with others to subject us to a jurisdiction foreign to our constitution, and unacknowledged by our laws; giving his Assent to their Acts of pretended Legislation: For quartering large bodies of armed troops among us. (Emphasis supplied).

In my view, there are two notions at work here: first, the British constitution and the laws enshrining the Rights of Englishmen from 1215-1776 did not permit unrepresentative legislation especially as concerned property rights. But the second notion was clearly stated by Thomas Jefferson in the above-underlined phrase: large bodies (organized units) of armed men among free citizens was an inherent threat to liberty.

For this reason, arguably, on both sides of the Atlantic there were no police forces or other organized professional bodies of armed men vested with the duty to keep order within the United Kingdom or the United States. Colonies like Ireland and Jamaica were not free and, thus, there were troops or other organized armed bodies present. This situation lasted until the modern area. The first police force organized in the UK came into existence in 1829 in London. It was organized by future British Home Secretary and future Prime Minister Sir Robert Peel. By the end of the following decade, all boroughs in England had police forces and all counties were authorized to create them. The police were regularly unarmed throughout most of the 19th century, despite routine violence against the constables and officers.

The reason? Free people feared the government would use armed bodies of men to oppress them. They did not care whether these bodies were actually soldiers or policemen or something else. Whenever permanent bodies of armed men were present, they knew there was a danger to liberty for all.

Fast forward a hundred years or so, and the citizen is confronted by vastly changed circumstances. Beginning, arguably, with the Drug Wars of the 1970's, the federal government began importing more and more of the national security apparatus for domestic use against U.S. citizens. DEA, ATF, FBI, and other federal government agencies increasingly targeted American citizens on American soil. Yes, these citizens were suspected of committing crimes. This was not a situation of wide scale monitoring of the citizen body irrespective of suspicion of crime (on that practice, see below). Most of the crimes related to drugs. A generation ago these would have been local policing matters or FBI matters once they crossed state lines. Federalization of the Drug Wars changed all of that.

The tragedy which took place on September 11, 2001, accelerated domestic targeting of U.S. citizens by the federal government. With the PATRIOT Act and other legislation, the federal government's powers to surveil, detain and prosecute persons in the United States outside the common law judicial channels (i.e., a court open to the public), were increased.

From the 1970's until now the number of secret prisons in America has risen. These include illegal alien detention centers as well as more secure facilities located throughout the United States. The excuse that the only detainees are foreigners neither absolves the federal government from this breach of the U.S. Constitution, nor allays the reasonable fears of citizens concerned about their own liberties.

In 1978, Congress created a new federal court called the Foreign Intelligence Surveillance Court ("FISA") specifically to oversee warrant applications and approvals for surveillance of foreign nationals within the United States who were suspected of spying. Between 1979 and 2004, the FISA granted more than 18,000 warrants to surveil persons inside the United States. Between 2004 and 2012, FISA granted almost the same number of warrant requests. Through the lifetime of this court, they have turned down almost no requests.

This court is significant in the context of the loss of liberty for several reasons. First, it functions entirely ex parte: only the government officials making the request and the judge or judges are present. Further, the court's procedures and internal rules are all secret. There is no third party monitoring going on. There is no accountability for getting things wrong and trampling on the rights of U.S. citizens and nationals. Obviously, the existence of FISA and its procedures that violate the common law are threats to Americans' liberty.

During the last fifteen years, other instances of unlawful surveillance and monitoring came to light through the press. Thanks to Edward Snowden, U.S. citizens now know the federal government has been and continues to obtain and store large amounts of information about them. And it has nothing to do with an individual being suspected of committing a crime. Certainly no warrants have been issued to authorize this behavior, yet it continues.

The federal government is not the only bad actor in this modern farce of liberty. State and local law enforcement, increasingly, are using sophisticated technology to monitor their fellow citizens who possess all of the same rights. Much of this technology is located on or directed at highways and other transportation infrastructure. But this hardly makes it reasonable or good. Gone are the days celebrated in the *Dukes of Hazzard*, one of my favorite TV shows growing up, in which well-meaning "good ole boys" zoom past a dozing sheriff's deputy slouched in an old car. Radar, military vehicles, aircraft, GPS, cellular networks, ubiquitous public surveillance cameras, mandatory facial recognition, biometric tracking - all are being brought to bear on U.S. citizens inside of America, whom the government is **required** to presume to be innocent until proven guilty by a jury of his or her peers in a public court. And when law enforcement gets it wrong, the injured citizen or surviving family members have no recourse against these government agents. How can liberty exist in such an environment?

The Destruction of Privacy

Step Four: The destruction of privacy. Another necessary step on the Road to Slavery is the destruction of privacy. Privacy is a necessary part of human dignity. Unlike animals, human beings require the ability to shut the world (including the government) out from a certain physical, emotional, and psychological space. This permits some of the higher functions of mankind to occur: leisure, play, reflection, worship, meditation, contemplation, innovation. These functions further distinguish us from animals.

The Founding Fathers believed this. And they believed they had a right to privacy. Legal antecedents support their opinions. In 1627, Parliament passed and presented to King Charles I the Petition of Right. Parliament passed this bill to check certain unlawful actions of the king in his attempts to raise funds and govern the country without Parliament's approval. This petition, to which King Charles gave the royal assent, re-established four principles of law now deemed axiomatic throughout the English-speaking world: (1) no taxation without representation; (2) the loss of life, liberty or property may only occur by judgment of one's peers according to the law of the land and not according to martial law or summarily; (3) citizens shall not be forced to quarter soldiers or marines; (4) executive authorities may not grant exemptions for violations of the law of the land or suspend the law, but must prosecute offenders of that law whomsoever they be.

Totalitarian governments need to destroy privacy. The rationale is two-fold: first, all citizens are deemed to be threats to the existing power structure. They must be constantly surveilled and regularly investigated. They also need to be kept in line through intimidation. The existence of privacy would mean that citizens could go to a place, as it were, to escape from the continuous presence of government and its invidious communication. Obviously then this could never be allowed to happen.

Secondly, privacy must be destroyed because it confers dignity upon individuals. Recall that the underlying government purpose behind totalitarian government is to make people better. In order to do so the government must have total control of the citizenry. There must be no place government agents cannot go and no information they cannot obtain. By whatever means. For the good of the people. If certain individuals stand in the way they must be dealt with. Swiftly. To keep the others in line.

No image of everyday life under a totalitarian regime is more telling than the breadline: waiting in line for hours to arrive at the head of the line in order to select some of what remains of government-chosen products and to purchase them at a government-fixed price. Misery is a breadline.

The most painful part of the death of privacy is the part we private individuals help to destroy it. Just ask yourself, when is the last time you turned off social media? How did your "friends" respond? Were they accepting of your right to be left alone, even by those who love you? Or did they criticize you? Make you feel like you were missing out? Make you feel like you were letting them down by not displaying every moment of your private lives to the scrutiny of others?

Do you remember when MTV came out with the series, *The Real World*, in the early 1990's? Ever the trend-setter, MTV created a new paradigm for entertainment that remains current more than a quarter century later. Witness both the hit British TV serieses *Love Island* and *Big Brother*. Who could miss that global entertainment phenomenon brought to us by the entire Kardashian family? (Does Kim have a billion followers yet?)

Back to *The Real World*. The premise was a group of strangers living together in a house in N.Y. for six months. Virtually all aspects of their lives that occured in the house were filmed: from the mundane to the glorious; from the painful to the ridiculous. It was all provided to the viewer seemingly uncut and natural.

Why was it called the Real World? I do not know. But I cannot pass on the significance of the title, especially as it sheds light on our current media-driven environment. Did the producers call it the Real World because they were attempting to present real, unscripted, uncut slices of life for the viewer to ingest? Or did the lives of the persons on the series become *real* in some sense because everything was filmed? As if the viewer's participation was what made it real life rather than just a bunch of actors in a TV show. As if viewing - media consumption - created something real.

Fast forward to our era *when even governmental officials take government action or communicate government policy in a*

Tweet!!???!!! "They cannot be serious!" some level-headed person must be thinking. But maybe the official thought, "Unless it's on social media it's not real".

This is the Real World. Everyone is being filmed all the time. Everyone is being identified, tracked, analyzed, and stored. Everyone can participate in this borderless identity and information exchange. You can switch off. But you can never leave.

The Collapse of Separation of Powers

The penultimate step on the Road to Slavery is the collapse of separation of powers. We owe our understanding of the importance of separation of powers to a free-spirited 18th century French nobleman, lawyer and judge named Charles de Secondat, Baron de Montesquieu. His magnum opus, *De l'Esprit des Loix* (The Spirit of the Laws), is one of the most important treatises on political theory ever written. It was published in 1748. Arguably, Montesquieu's writings were the greatest foreign influence on the Founding Fathers who wrote our constitution.

Montesquieu theorized that all government power could be divided into three separate powers: the power to make laws (legislation); the power to carry out laws, make war or peace, and regulate foreign trade (the executive); and the power to punish crimes and regulate the citizens' disputes (the judiciary). Liberty, according to Montesquieu, was a state of mind. But it was produced by a constitution (government structure) and laws (including liberties, ancient customs and rights) that separated the powers of government among different bodies. Critically, according to Montesquieu, whenever one of the powers assumed or encroached on another power, liberty would be extinguished and tyranny or despotism would result.

Ironically for a Frenchman, Montesquieu's model for the separation of powers was the English constitution as it existed in the late seventeenth and early eighteenth centuries. This was before the exaltation of His Majesty's First Minister into an elected quasi-monarch and the development of organized, modern political parties. Back then, the Sovereign did really rule "in Parliament". He or she could declare war, make peace, receive embassies, and regulate trade but the sovereign could not levy a single cent (other than via the crown's enormous landholdings throughout Britain) without the consent of the Peers and Commons of the Realm. The sovereign could prorogue Parliament; the sovereign could refuse to call Parliament (French Kings Louis XIII through Louis XVI, in a similar context, did not call the French *assemblée des Etats* to secure their finances and help regulate the Kingdom of France from 1614 until the fateful year of 1789, choosing instead to rule *absolutely*); but the sovereign could not get any public money without Parliament.

Unlike their French cousins, the Stuart Kings of Britain could not last without a Parliament for more than eleven years. In the first instance (1629-1640), it led to civil war and the only judicial regicide in English history. In the second instance (when Charles II dissolved Parliament in 1679 and did not call it again through his death in 1685) this unconstitutional state of affairs did not last a decade. By a Parliament-inspired coup d'état in 1688, King James II fled Britain, was deemed to have "abandoned the throne", and was replaced by his daughter and son-in-law (who himself was a grandson of King Charles I by his daughter Mary). They co-reigned as King William and Queen Mary. Through this means, Parliament not only returned to the national stage but also moved to its center. The Bill of Rights was passed the following year, which when it was signed by King William and Queen Mary effectively turned England into a constitutional monarchy - a hybrid government where the sovereign's powers or roles are in some way regulated by another representative body. The Bill of Rights secured for Englishmen the following rights that all American civics students should recognize: freedom of speech (within Parliament); the right to bear arms (Protestants only, please); freedom from cruel and unusual punishment; *freedom from excessive bail;* no taxation without representation; free elections; no deprivation of property without trial (due process); *freedom from standing armies during peacetime.*

The Bill of Rights also fixed the succession of the Crown by barring Roman Catholics and debarring the heirs of King William's body in the event Queen Mary died without issue (as she would tragically five years later) in favor of her sister the Queen of Denmark and *her* heirs. And within twenty-five years, the legitimate Stuart line (at least under English law) died out. This thoroughly British family was replaced by a thoroughly German one, who in due time gave to America her last king - George III.

In my opinion, of the three powers of government, the one Montesquieu feared the most was the legislative power. I say this because Montesquieu concluded that the corruption of the legislature alone would destroy liberty. Here is what he had to say:

> If the legislative body was once corrupted, the evil
> would be past all remedy. When different legislative
> bodies succeed one another, the people who have
> a bad opinion of that which is actually sitting, may
> reasonably entertain some hopes of the next: *But
> were it to be always the same body, the people,
> upon seeing it once corrupted, would no longer
> expect any good from its laws; and of course they
> would either become desperate, or fall into a state
> of indolence.*

This was not the only danger Montesquieu perceived from the collapse of separation of government powers:

> Were the legislative body to be a considerable time without meeting, this would likewise put an end to liberty. For one of these two things would naturally follow; either that there would be no longer any legislative resolutions, and then the state would fall into anarchy; or that these resolutions would be taken by the executive power, which would render it absolute.

The ideal circumstances for the collapse of one of the fundamental powers of government or of its assumption by another branch of government is during a public health crisis. No, I am not simply taking advantage of the current coronavirus climate to score a cheap shot against the Democratic Party - the party responsible for needlessly shutting down the U.S. economy during the spring of 2020. The widespread presence of an invisible, lethal pathogen is the perfect circumstance for generating the *fear* necessary for free people to be willing to overlook the constitutional and legal separation of government power in an effort to be made to *feel* safe.

Unfortunately for myself and my fellow New Yorkers, the best example of how the collapse of separation of powers destroys liberty is that of our home state in 2020 during the coronavirus crisis.

Before we examine the government's unconstitutional and unlawful actions ostensibly related to fighting this infection, it is important to show the actual impact of the virus on New York's people. The facts are so shockingly different from what the media tells us, that I will let them speak for themselves. The source of the statistics below, according to Google, is Wikipedia and the New York Times news agency.

At the time I am writing this in mid-August, New York continues to lead all fifty states with the most coronavirus related deaths at over 32,339. The next closest state, New Jersey, does not have half that number - 15,893. However, it should also be pointed out that of those deaths, more than 23,000 occurred in N.Y.C alone.

For those readers who do not know, New York has sixty-two counties. New York City is spread throughout five separate counties. For the remaining fifty-seven counties in New York State, as of August 15th, there is no single county in which the total number of deaths exceeds 2,200 persons over more than six months. What is worse (for the government's case) is that only three counties outside of New York City have a total number of deaths above 1,000. Two of those three counties border N.Y.C.

More bad news for the government: only eight counties have a death rate greater than 100 but less than 1,000. What does that mean? It means that in forty-six of New York's sixty-two counties (74%), less than 100 people have died from COVID-19 and related complications. These counties make up at least half of the landmass of the state. Further, twenty-one of New York's sixty-two counties (33.87%) have a death rate in the single digits and one county has suffered no deaths from the coronavirus.

In sum, New York leads the nation in coronavirus-related deaths with over 32,000 as of August 15th. But 74% of New York's counties have not experienced 100 total deaths. And more than one-third of New York's counties have a death rate in the single digits or below.

First, let's stop, bow our knees and thank God Almighty that the toll was not worse.

Next, because we now know the truth, we must ask some hard questions. Of ourselves, of the media who continue to cover the coronavirus crisis and continue to ignore (at best) relevant facts like the death rate outside of N.Y.C and neighboring counties, and then of our state government. This, like voting, is a duty free citizens have to our government and to our society.

What was the response of New York's government to the novel coronavirus?

An unconstitutional power grab. Here is how the state government stole our freedom:

On March 7th, Governor Andrew Cuomo issued Executive Order 202. This order declared in its first substantive paragraph that "a disaster is impending in New York state, for which the affected local governments are unable to respond adequately." This finding was based on Section 28 of Article 2-B of the Executive Law. Further, the order declared "a State disaster emergency <u>for the entire State of New York</u>." (Emphasis supplied). Lastly, the order *ipse dixit* declared it would expire on September 7th - six months later.

Let us examine this paragraph more closely. First, the action taken was an Executive Order. It was not a law passed by the people's representatives in both the State Assembly and Senate and signed by the governor. It was not a regulation promulgated by a state agency through power granted to it by the legislature through a law signed by the governor. It was an act of executive authority akin to exercising police power. Second, New York Executive Law, Article 2-B, Section 28 (State declaration of disaster emergency), purports to grant the governor the authority to identify that "a disaster has occurred or may be imminent for which local governments are unable to respond adequately". But the text of Section 28 only discusses one specific type of disaster: "a radiological accident." The current text of Section 28 may be found online. Third, while Section 28 does permit the governor to issue an Executive Order that lasts for up to six months, it does require that the order "shall include a description of the disaster, and the affected area."

Meanwhile, Section 20(2)(a) of Article 2-B of the New York Executive Law, contains the definition of disaster. This section has been amended four times since the law was originally passed in 1978.

Prior to the last amendment, the definition of disaster was:

> "occurrence or imminent threat of wide spread or severe damage, injury, or loss of life or property resulting from any natural or man-made causes, including, but not limited to, fire, flood, earthquake, hurricane, tornado, high water, landslide, mudslide, wind, storm, wave action, volcanic activity, epidemic, air contamination, terrorism, cyber event, blight, drought, infestation, explosion, radiological accident, nuclear, chemical, biological, or bacteriological release, water contamination, bridge failure or bridge collapse."

In the current version, the legislature added "impending or urgent" with respect to the threatened activity, and "disease outbreak" among the types of causes triggering executive authority to act.

When was this changed? *Four days before Governor Cuomo issued Executive Order 202!* What non-New Yorkers may not know, but may find relevant to this part of the analysis, is that both the State Assembly and the Senate are controlled by the Democratic Party. Thus it may have been that Governor Cuomo and his fellow Democratic leaders in the legislature got together and stacked the deck, as it were. For some reason the legislature saw fit to change the definition of "disaster" just before Governor Cuomo took action against the coronavirus. There was no effective political opposition to this change. And, apparently, there was not even time to seek public comment about the proposed changes.

Thus this change and the actions that followed which were based on the change were *unrepresentative.*

Pursuant to this alleged authority, Governor Cuomo issued many Executive Orders addressing a variety of activities. He has unilaterally suspended or changed numerous laws in New York State. Governor Cuomo has suspended or changed provisions of election law, childcare law, anti-bribery [sic] law, residency requirements for certain government appointments, healthcare law, public education law, the treatment of persons with developmental disabilities, public utility law, and laws or regulations governing other aspects of a free society. The website Politico.com has reported on this.

What about the other two branches of state government? What were their responses to the coronavirus crisis? Both the legislature and the state court systems virtually collapsed. The legislature suspended its session from April 2 until May 26; they left themselves three days to finish their legislative activity <u>for the year</u>. Meanwhile, the state courts shut themselves down. From March 22 until May 25, an order from the state's chief administrative judge barred all new filings in state court in "nonessential" matters. Even the electronic filing system - which a litigant's lawyer can access from his or her office or home - was shut down. While some judicial figures might claim that the courts were not shut down (because, for example, family court emergency proceedings could still be initiated) that was not this author's experience.

In Broome County, New York, where I was living during the coronavirus crisis, I attempted to file two new lawsuits. I claimed that each were essential matters as defined by an Administrative Order issued by the chief administrative judge. In New York, new lawsuits are filed with the County Clerk's office. That office's personnel refused to file either of my lawsuits. Their explanation was that the courts were shut down and not accepting new civil actions.

The reality of what happened is obvious: the legislature and the courts were comfortable allowing just the executive to remain open and functioning. In so doing, they created circumstances in which American citizens were subject to executive action without recourse to the courts for relief. They also permitted (and are still permitting at the time I am writing this) the executive to legislate on education law, healthcare law and any other area he sees fit. This was the real reign of terror.

This is not constitutional. The U.S. Constitution and the N.Y.S Constitution both provide for separation of powers. This is designed to protect the rights and liberties of American citizens. Separation of powers is not about convenience; it is not subordinate to public safety. In the words of Montesquieu, it is about preventing tyranny and despotism. In New York, what Montesquieu foresaw occurred: the legislature super-empowered the executive and then ceased meeting for almost two months. And the courts were shut down. The result? ***Absolute power.***

The most bitter part of this unconstitutional experience is that it could have been avoided. Not because President Trump could or should have done something different, although that is true. But because Governor Cuomo could have confined his unconstitutional mandates to the parts of the state most severely impacted by the coronavirus.

Recall that in August 2020, 74% of New York's counties still had not experienced even 100 COVID-19-related deaths. More than one-third of New York's counties still had a single digit death rate from COVID-19 after six months of supposed pandemic. Thus Governor Cuomo's actions as applied to an entire state are completely disproportionate.

Unconstitutional, unlawful, unrepresentative.

Dictators always make someone feel safe. They never make anyone feel free. Except government agents breaking the laws and violating individuals' rights.

Indefinite Equals Permanent

The terminal step is when the dictators make the new state of affairs permanent. Wise dictators employ others to call for this fatal change. Regardless of who makes the call, it will inevitably be made.

Thankfully, we have not reached this step yet in 2020. But it could be just around the corner. Dictators possess a variety of mechanisms to make this happen. In New York, Governor Cuomo's unconstitutional rule by fiat has temporary expiration dates which he can unilaterally extend indefinitely. While Executive Order 202 is set to expire on September 7th, subsequent orders have already been extended past their thirty day limits. The Executive Orders extending Executive Orders bear the title, "Continuing Temporary Suspension and Modification of Laws Relating to the Disaster Emergency." The statistics above show that outside of N.Y.C and two counties that border it (plus one other), the coronavirus has not caused an emergency. Thus there is no justification for one-man rule throughout most of the state. To the extent there was a disaster for most of the state it was government-made. President Reagan warned us about those types of events.

Another mechanism is suspending elections. Thankfully, again, in our country federal elections occur on a date determined by Congress. It cannot be unilaterally changed by either the U.S. President or by state governors. It is fitting of the age in which we live when liberty is under threat, that both President Trump and state governors are making noise about suspending, postponing or otherwise altering Election Day. This is both unnecessary and disturbing. The states have months to put various safety measures in place in order to ensure the people can safely exercise their sovereign right and sovereign duty to vote on November 3rd, 2020. Failure to do this would be grossly negligent. Intentional failure to do this would be treason.

Remember: Hitler was elected. Mussolini was elected. Napoleon Bonaparte was elected. Napoleon III was elected. Julius Caesar was elected. The people chose their dictators.

Conclusion

Will the American Republic (Government) endure? This is not the final, fatal question, which is, Will the American republic (the *form* of government) endure? The world is familiar enough with the tactics of tyrants to know that a Republic in name only, like a marriage in name only, is a fraud. Many exist. We must stand up and fight for our republic so that it does not become one of them.

From where I sit today I can see how much ground we have lost in the battle for freedom-equality. We are no longer the country in which almost everyone has a decent opportunity to make his or her life both materially and qualitatively better. We are no longer the society that recognizes that all of its members have the same rights and that foreigners among us should be welcomed and deserve to be treated with dignity. We are no longer free like we once were. This represents moral failures as well as persistent political problems.

The Baby Boom and the government-underwritten Higher Education revolution expanded individual freedom. These phenomena transformed American society and work post World War II by giving more knowledge to more Americans of both sexes than ever before. More wealth was created and owned by persons who did not belong to wealthy families than ever before in human history. The frontiers of science yielded to the will of man; we put two humans on the Moon. What problems could we not solve? What would we invent next?

But we were building a monster, a freak of arrogant, selfish, self-destructive consumerism that threatens to consume us and destroy the earth. We gained the whole world, but lost our souls. This explains the low level of civic and community engagement in the face of near-constant social media connectivity. We are isolated and desensitized to what is happening down the street from our homes, let alone across town or the state or the country or the world. If it is a problem and it does not concern us or those we love, we do not care. Period. But if it is funny and shareable on social media then, well, we are willing to be entertained. We do not know who our neighbors are but we know every detail of the rift between Harry and Meghan and the British Royal Family. Further, our neighbors change too frequently through death and relocation to form relationships of growth.

This is a recipe for the collapse of civil society. In such a picture, the only constant, the only savior as it were, is the Government. Already, many Americans with good intentions are calling for the Government to step up to the plate.

We must resist this call with every ounce of courage, intellect, love and will that we possess. And we must resist this call together.

The truth is that our spirits are in bondage; the American spirit is in chains again. We forged the shackles that we wear. We need to repent of our sins, addictions and self-destructive pleasures. We as a nation and as individuals need to cry out to God. Only the Lord Jesus Christ can get us out of this mess we have made of ourselves, our families, our communities and our land.

The creation of a new nation called "American" was an act of faith; faith is one of our most important forgotten values. The Land of America birthed these United States in 1776 in blood and lead with the values of life, liberty and the pursuit of happiness. But those first Americans had faith - faith that if they could remain free, they could work to build a better tomorrow for themselves and their posterity. It would necessarily take sacrifice, but they were willing to make it. In 2020, however, life increasingly is under fire, under the pill, under the knife throughout our country. Liberty has become a question too often answered only by many dollars and slick lawyers. Happiness, however, is another matter.

Happiness is alive and well in twenty-first century America. When have we ever had more TV channels, sports leagues, suburban tracts, movies, video games, toys, craft beers, cheap food? Porn is legal and ubiquitous. One can gamble online. And we have drugs to treat all of these addictions. We have never been so fat, happy, soulless and dying.

Politically, the pursuit of happiness illustrates a major success of American society itself during the past fifty years. During that time, American society moved from Keeping up with the Joneses to Keeping up with the Joneses, Patels, Parks, Shahs, Wangs, Millers, Murphys, O'Neills, Khans, Lees, DeFranciscos, Garcias y Gonzalezes, de Souzas, Smiths, Johnsons and Davises. *All of these families are pursuing the same thing*: happiness. Most Americans accept this race. This social revolution was economic, academic, specialized, and successful. It was also numerous if still concentrated geographically along the coasts and in inland metropolises. One path to future political success in America is putting all of these families under one roof with a common set of political objectives, such as protecting property rights while expanding economic opportunities. Such a party would never lose a democratic election for any office in the land except by undemocratic means.

But this explosion of happiness came at what cost to the soul of the American nation? Isn't there more to life in America than being happy?

I answer, "Yes." So did the founding patriots I mentioned earlier, as well as the generation that fought to end slavery through our Civil War, the generation mobilised successfully to fight totalitarian evil in Europe, Asia, and Africa in the 1940's, the generation under arms in our military today. They *believed* there was something *in* America worth dying for. And that thing is freedom and that action is faith.

As Albert Camus said, "Freedom is the chance to be better." Either the Government can defend your freedom and you do the rest, or the Government can give you the better, but it (bureaucrats and politicians and experts) gets to call the shots. All of them.

On November 3rd, 2020, choose accordingly.

Donald Trump is trying to restore the birthright of opportunity that is the possession of our nation. He is not trying to take away any American's freedom. His administration clearly demonstrated that through his policies. He alone was willing to fight China on unfair trade and did so. He worked hard to improve opportunities for businesses and for workers. During the first three years of his administration, despite constant opposition from the House Democratic Leadership, Donald Trump helped create the strongest American economy in more than fifty years.

And then 2020 presented America and the world with a new challenge. No, I do not mean the novel coronavirus. I mean the challenge of domestic tyranny in the West. Eight Democratic state governors and one Republican decided that they had the power to unilaterally shut down the world's most powerful economy. They decided that free people had given them the right to decide which businesses could stay open and which the government could order to close. Without being asked directly. Not even at a press conference beforehand. (Is anyone surprised that the businesses deemed "essential" are heavily unionized or large corporations, while the "nonessential" ones are the small businesses that make up the bulk of the private sector?)

The idea that free and law-abiding people can be involuntarily shut up in their homes without representation - i.e., without a legislature elected by and accountable to those people voting to change the law - is ludicrous. Even temporarily for, as I discussed earlier in this book, temporary becomes indefinite; indefinite becomes permanent. No democracy can run on unconstitutional exigencies for long and freedom be safe, even during a war. The American republic is no exception.

What of the opposition? Listen carefully to what they are saying. What do you hear, reader? Endless superlatives of *happiness* brought to you free of charge by the Government. Free healthcare. Free jobs. Free vacations. Free abortion. Free, free, free.

How will all of this happiness be provided? Not by individual work, the backbone of not just our economy but our culture; economic opportunity brought more people to America's shores than any other cause. Rather, the Left would provide endless happiness through ceaseless, limitless government action.

More than 180 years ago, that prescient political science genius from France, Alexis de Tocqueville, foresaw this problem and warned posterity: "The American republic will endure until the day

Congress discovers that it can bribe the public with the public's money."

The Left is trying to bribe us with our own money to get what they are after.

They are also offering a new narrative of American exceptionalism - the exceptionalism of guilt. Endless condemnation for every racist thought and deed that ever happened ... before most of us were born. (Based on U.S. census data from 2019, of the 330 million Americans alive today, more than 70% were not alive prior to the Voting Rights Act of 1965 (which I support)). Notice how much rhetoric the Left wastes on circumstances outside of the memories of their audience.

Those acts may not be memories of most Americans, but they can still stir the emotions of almost all of us.

The Left is correct to condemn the blatant racist killings of innocent Black men occurring throughout the country. Period.

But their proposed solutions to this problem would leave Black people and other Americans more vulnerable instead of making Black people safer. Accountability in courts of law is what is required, not dismantling police forces or making them creatures of public committees.

Yet I am talking about a presidential election, and policing is a state issue. Is the Left proposing to federalize police regulation in America? Are they aware of the precedents of national police forces? Do they realize that smaller, locally accountable police forces (which is not what they mean by Defund the police; just ask their anarchist friends!) promote liberty and law and order?

What is their real game?

Ask New York Governor Andrew Cuomo. Or rather, download and listen to ten or so of his COVID-19 press conferences. Listen as he reasonably articulates why he had to take away New Yorker's freedoms unconstitutionally and unrepresentatively. Listen as he mocks and condemns any dissent, any contrary point of view to his own as either unscientific or irrelevant.

Doesn't he look good doing it? Doesn't he sound reasonable?

This is the face of tyranny. It shows us what the Left is after: total state power.

Resist them at all costs!

Made in the USA
Middletown, DE
02 November 2020